PRAGUE CASTLE

DETAILED GUIDE

PRAGUE
PUBLISHING HOUSE
OF JIŘÍ POLÁČEK
1994

CONTENTS

© Text and Drawings: Petr Chotěbor, 1994
© Translation: Joy Turner-Kadečková, 1994
© Photographs: Barbara Hucková, Miroslav Hucek, 1994
ISBN 80-901544-4-1, (čes. ISBN 80-901544-2-5, něm. 80-901544-3-3)

FOREWORD

Prague Castle has gazed down on the River Vltava for a full eleven centuries. It has its own order and rhythm of life to which normal human criteria do not apply.

During its long existence an endless number of people has passed this way who ruled, held office, worked hard or, on the contrary, enjoyed life in a carefree manner or merely looked around curiously here. People come and go and only very few leave their permanent mark here. Even those who devoted their whole life to the Castle were actually here for a short time only.

The Castle has naturally undergone changes even though as regards size it has remained the same since the time of its foundation. Periods of flourish and splendour alternated with feverish building activity, war events or fires and bad times of oblivion and disrepair. The Castle gradually ceased to be a strategic military point and its importance as the centre and symbol of the Czech state grew. And Prague Castle has been this centre, the seat of the head of state or at least the central state administration throughout its existence.

So many significant events in Czech history are directly connected with Prague Castle! So many times did it witness the installation of princes or the election of kings, so many times did it experience solemn coronations and so many important decisions were taken by the ruler or the Provincial Diet here! And it must not be forgotten that the Castle has also been the scene of historic events of European importance – indeed, on two occasions in its history it was the seat of the Roman emperor!

Here each one of the visitors who pass through the Castle in millions every year can find what he is looking for here: an authentic historical environment, valuable architectural monuments, rich art collections, the majestic silence of cathedral interiors, beautiful and romantic corners, interesting exhibitions and concerts, the effective sight of the changing of the Castle guard, relaxation in gardens or an unforgettable view of the city. Apart from all these things, however, he can also come across visible signs of efforts to preserve this unique area.

THE DEVELOPMENT OF PRAGUE CASTLE

Prague Castle at the Time of the Přemyslid Dynasty

The Beginnings of Prague Castle. The past of Prague Castle reaches back to the 9th century. According to the results of archeological research and the oldest written sources it is estimated that it was founded by the first historically documented prince of the Přemyslid dynasty, Bořivoj. The site which he chose corresponded to all the requirements imposed on the position of a castle site: it afforded a good view, had natural protection and was accessible at the same time. In the south-east a long and narrow rocky ridge sloped sheerly down to the valley of the River Vltava and in the north to the gorge of the little River Brusnice. In the west it was separated from the remainder of the headland by a natural furrow.

The medieval Castle site. Soon after its foundation Prague Castle had the typical appearance of a medieval castle site. Its whole periphery was fortified by a ditch and a mound of earth and stones, which was strengthened inside with a structure of trunks and branches. Even at that time the Castle was as big as it is today – big enough to hold a lot of inhabitants, who lived in small houses of the wooden frame type.

The first churches. Bořivoj I was the first Přemyslid prince to accept Christianity. He founded the first churches in Bohemia, the oldest of them being St. Clement's Rotunda, which he had built at his original seat at Levý Hradec. A little later the first church at Prague Castle, the Church of Our Lady, originated. At the same time it was the first building in the locality to be built of stone.

St. George's Church. The second church at Prague Castle was founded about 920 on the site of the present St. George's Basilica by Bořivoj's son – Prince Vratislav I.

St. Vitus's Church. The impulse for the building of the third church at Prague Castle in 925 was given by Bořivoj's grandson and Vratislav's son Václav. It was designed as a monumental rotunda with four apses and consecrated to St. Vitus. Three years after the murder of Prince Václav the rotunda became the place of his burial, respected in the course of all later reconstructions.

The Prague bishopric. In 973, at the time of Prince Boleslav, the Prague bishopric was established with Prague's first bishop, Dětmar, at its head. The stone seat of the bishop with an adjoining chapel was built on an elevated position on the castle site (now the Old Deanery in the Third Courtyard) at the end of the 10th or the beginning of the 11th century.

The first convent. The consent of the pope in respect of the founding of the Prague bishopric, but also the first convent in Bohemia, was gained in 973 by Mlada, sister of Prince Boleslav II. The first abbess of the convent, built near St. George's Church for the nuns of the Benedictine order, was Mlada herself.

Battles for the Castle. The early 11th century is recorded in history as a restless period: Several rivals competed for the rule over the country and thus also for the Castle. In 1003 the Castle even fell into foreign hands, being occupied by the troops of the Polish ruler Boleslav Chrabrý. One year later, with the help of the German king Henry II, the Přemyslids regained the Castle. In later years Prince Břetislav I was defeated by the Emperor Henry III, whose troops besieged Prague Castle and set it on fire in 1041. Břetislav's humiliating defeat resulted in the total reconstruction of the fortifications of the Castle in the following years.

The throne of princes. Cosmos's chronicle describing the election of Břetislav I tells us details about this ceremony: in order that the election might be valid and acknowledged, the prince had to be installed, i.e., seated on a stone throne. It evidently stood on the area of the square U svatého Jiří of the present.

St. Vitus's Basilica. Břetislav's son Spytihněv II had the St. Vitus's Rotunda founded by Václav demolished. It no longer sufficed to hold the believers and in 1060 a bigger church was founded in the form of a basilica with two choirs. The construction work was continued by his successor Vratislav II, who in 1085 became the first Czech king and was crowned in the basilica. However, it was not until it had been wholly completed in 1096 that the church, damaged by fire in 1091, was consecrated. From the time of Vratislav, who moved to Vyšehrad, the Castle ceased to be the seat of the ruler until the mid-12th century.

Vitus, Wenceslas and Adalbert (Vít, Václav and Vojtěch). The main Castle church was connected with the names of three saints. St. Vitus

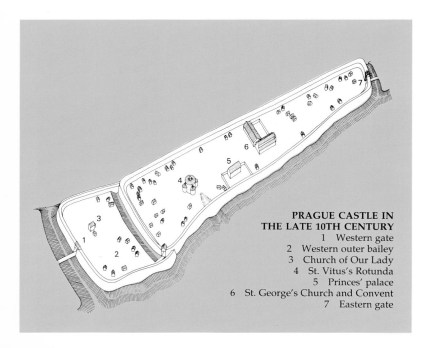

PRAGUE CASTLE IN
THE LATE 10TH CENTURY
1   Western gate
2   Western outer bailey
3   Church of Our Lady
4   St. Vitus's Rotunda
5   Princes' palace
6   St. George's Church and Convent
7   Eastern gate

was the first to be revered here: Prince Václav received a bone from his arm as a gift representing a rare relic from the Emperor Jindřich Ptáčník from the Saxon treasure and placed it in the just finished rotunda. Prince Václav himself became the principal saint and patron of the Czechs: his tabernacle has remained in St. Vitus's Cathedral to the present. St. Adalbert, the second Czech bishop, was killed during

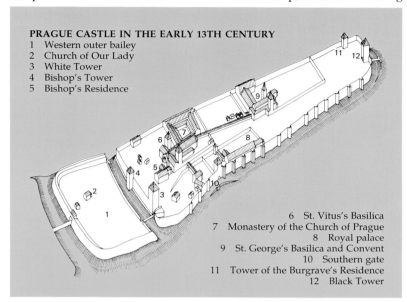

PRAGUE CASTLE IN THE EARLY 13TH CENTURY
1   Western outer bailey
2   Church of Our Lady
3   White Tower
4   Bishop's Tower
5   Bishop's Residence

6   St. Vitus's Basilica
7   Monastery of the Church of Prague
8   Royal palace
9   St. George's Basilica and Convent
10   Southern gate
11   Tower of the Burgrave's Residence
12   Black Tower

his mission journey to the Baltic Prussians, but his remains, brought back to the Castle from his military expedition by Břetislav I in 1039, were buried in the western, tower-shaped annex of St. Vitus's Rotunda.

The Romanesque Castle. One of the most extensive reconstructions of Prague Castle is connected with the name of Soběslav I. After 1135 he had a new stone wall built on the site of the several times destroyed and rebuilt fortification mound. It surrounded the whole inner Castle, only the western outer bailey still being protected by a mound and a ditch. The Castle wall, which was up to 14 metres in height, was strengthened with four square towers (the White Tower by the western gate, the Black Tower with the gate from the east, the southern tower and the tower of the Burgrave's Residence). The southern part of the wall was fortified with solid turrets, the Princes' Palace, built at the same time, being connected with it. After Soběslav the Romanesque reconstruction was evidently completed by Prince, later King Vladislav II. In that period the castle site definitely gained the appearance of a medieval castle.

War damage. During the reign of Vladislav II the Castle was under siege and bombardment for five weeks by the troops of the apanage prince Konrád Znojemský. True, the Castle was successfully defended, but the damage brought about especially by the fires caused by missiles was so great that a number of buildings had to be repaired or rebuilt. The Castle was often besieged and conquered in constant struggles for the throne also during the last third of the 12th century, this period naturally being unfavourable for building activity.

The court of the last Přemyslids. More stable conditions were brought about by the rule of Přemysl Otakar I and Václav I in the first half of the 13th century. However, the appearance of the Castle did not undergo any great change. We know only of partial reconstructions in St. George's Convent and in the so-called monastery of the Church of Prague (in the chapter house attached to the Basilica of St. Vitus, St. Wenceslas and St. Adalbert). The Royal Palace was also reconstructed and the fortifications renewed at the time of Přemysl Otakar II. Nevertheless, the short period of flourish of the Czech Kingdom did not bring about any marked change in the appearance of the Castle itself.

Disasters and catastrophes. At the time when Václav II, not yet of age, was held captive in a predatory manner and the country was under the rule of Ota of Brandenburg Prague Castle was the victim of a big natural disaster. In 1280 it was damaged by a gale and heavy downpour which caused a landslide on the northern slope of the gorge of the River Brusnice. The fire which occurred at the Castle in 1303 caused great damage particularly to the Royal Palace. The disfavour of Fate culminated in 1306, when Václav II was treacherously murdered. This brought the Přemysl dynasty to an end on the male side.

c. 880	Founding of Prague Castle
Before 894	Founding of the Church of Our Lady
c. 920	Founding of St. George's Church
c. 925	Founding of St. Vitus's Rotunda
938	Bodily remains of Prince Václav transferred to the rotunda
973	Founding of the Prague bishopric and Benedictine convent attached to St. George's Church
1003	Occupation of the Castle by the Polish troops of Boleslav Chrabrý
1041	Siege of the Castle by imperial troops, damage by fire, commencement of Prince Břetislav I's reconstruction
1060	Founding of the Basilica of St. Vitus, St. Wenceslas and St. Adalbert
1091	Basilica damaged by fire
1096	Consecration of the renewed basilica
1135	Beginning of the Romanesque reconstruction of the Castle
1142	Siege of the Castle by the troops of Konrád Znojemský, damaged by fire
1280	Castle damaged by gales, downpours and a landslide
1303	Occurrence of fire at the Royal Palace

The Luxembourg Castle

The new dynasty. Two pretenders to the Czech throne tried to gain Prague Castle: Rudolph Hapsburg, son of the Emperor Albrecht, and Henry of Carinthia, consort of Anna Přemyslovna, daughter of Václav II. After the restless years when Bohemia was successively under the rule of one and then the other the Emperor Henry VII placed his son John on the Czech throne at the request of the Czech Diet. John of Luxembourg married the second daughter of Václav II, Eliška Přemyslovna, and in 1310, with the aid of Czech and imperial troops, ruled Prague and the Castle, which, however, was wholly uninhabitable at that time.

Charles IV the builder. John of Luxembourg did not devote great attention to the state of Prague Castle. It was finally his son – the later king and emperor Charles IV – who still as the Margrave of Moravia represented the king in his absence – that began a wide–scale reconstruction, in particular of the Royal Palace. He extended the old Romanesque building to the west as far as the southern gate, adding to the northen side a row of arcades which made it possible to widen the ground-plan for the reception hall on the first floor.

The builders of the Castle. Charles IV wanted to build a cathedral here after the model of French cathedrals. After the laying of the foundation stone of St. Vitus's Cathedral on 21. 11. 1344, during his stay at the Pope's seat in Avignon, he therefore sought as the first builder the experienced Matthias of Arras. In 1356 Peter Parler became the next builder of Prague's cathedral. Under his leadership a building and art workshop of European importance was built-up at the Castle. Peter Parler conceived not only the architecture (the Golden Portal, St. Wenceslas's Chapel and the vault of the high choir with the first net vault on the European continent), but also the decoration of the cathedral. For the transferred tombs of the Czech kings and princes the St. Vitus workshop produced really magnificent tombstones, the portrait gallery of the inner triforium also representing outstanding sculptural work.

Charles's imperial residence. Prague Castle continued to be Charles's seat also when he became the Czech king and later the Roman emperor as well after the death of John of Luxembourg. The building activity corresponded to the importance and glitter of the imperial residence. Numerous building works were also carried out in St. George's Convent. The fortifications of the Castle were thoroughly repaired and strengthened on the southern side with a parkan with a new ditch. The White and the Black Tower were provided with new roofs of gilded lead plates.

The Václav Wing. Most of the buildings continued during the reign of Charles's son, Václav IV. The Royal Palace gained two transverse wings and the former flat ceilings were replaced with vaults. Václav had the old Romanesque chapel in the reconstructed Royal Palace replaced with a spacious church consecrated to All Saints. During the reconstruction of the palace the king took up residence at the Royal Court in the Old Town and no longer lived permanently at the Castle. Building activity was suddenly brought to an end by his death and the outbreak of the Hussite wars.

Looting and destruction. At the beginning of the battles Prague Castle was looted by the inhabitants of Prague, later being opened to the garrison of the Emperor Zikmund due to the treachery the burgrave. After his hasty coronation in 1420 Zikmund left the country along with the coronation jewels. His garrison resisted siege for a year, the final occupation of the Castle by the people of Prague giving rise especially to the destruction of the churches and their decoration.

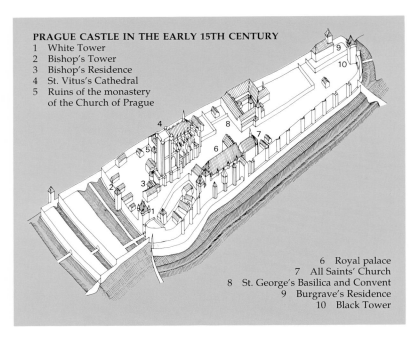

PRAGUE CASTLE IN THE EARLY 15TH CENTURY
1 White Tower
2 Bishop's Tower
3 Bishop's Residence
4 St. Vitus's Cathedral
5 Ruins of the monastery
   of the Church of Prague

6 Royal palace
7 All Saints' Church
8 St. George's Basilica and Convent
9 Burgrave's Residence
10 Black Tower

1333	Return of margoare Charles from France and commencement of the reconstruction of the Royal Palace
1344	Prague bishopric raised to an archbishopric, laying of the foundation stone of St. Vitus's Cathedral
1367	Consecration of St. Wenceslas's Chapel in the cathedral
1373	Transfer of the graves of Czech princes and kings
1382	Reconstruction of the Royal Palace, Václav IV moves his seat to the Royal Court in the Old Town
1385	Consecration of the completed choir of the cathedral
1392	Laying of the foundation stone of the nave
1396	Founding of the great steeple of the cathedral
1419	Outbreak of the Hussite unrests, interruption of building activity at the Castle
1420	Occupation of the Castle by the garrison of the Emperor Zikmund
1421	Capitulation of the garrison, occupation of the Castle by the people of Prague

The Jagiello Castle

The deserted Castle. A number of rulers alternated after the termination of the Hussite wars: the Emperor Zikmund, for a short time Albrecht of Austria, Ladislav Pohrobek and after him George of Poděbrady. However, none of them resided at the Castle. And, like them, the first ruler from the Jagiello dynasty of Poland – Vladislav – resided at the Royal Court in the town. It was finally the Prague uprisings in 1483 that compelled him to move to the then safer Castle, which gave rise to further building activity here.

New fortifications. After a whole century of falling into disrepair it was necessary to restore and newly fortify the seat of Czech kings. The then system of fortifications and towers no longer sufficed as means of protection against the effects of artillery, which underwent enormous development during the 15th century. Thus the king summoned Benedikt Ried mainly for their reconstruction. B. Ried strengthened the western entrance to the Castle with a new tower gateway, building a small residential palace next to it. The parkan on the southern side was supplemented with three semicircular cannon bastions, while the eastern gate was strengthened with a barbican with a small round tower. On the northern side, which was under the greatest threat of enemy artillery fire, he built a new parkan with three cannon towers, namely the Powder Tower or Mihulka, the new White Tower and Daliborka. The northern parkan was provided with a defence passage in which gunpowder was protected against moisture and the gunners covered behind loopholes with rotating wooden drums.

The works of Benedikt Ried. In the following years B. Ried proved himself to be an all-round architect. He rebuilt and enlarged the western wing of the Royal Palace, where Vladislav had already had an audience hall built (incorrectly called Vladislav's bedchamber). He inserted a new royal oratory in one of the chapels of the cathedral, on the level of the first floor connected with the Royal Palace.

The Vladislav Hall. Benedikt Ried's most important work was the new throne hall, still called the Vladislav Hall after the king who had it built. The architectect preserved only the peripheral walls of the reception floor of the palace from the time of Charles IV. He vaulted the hall with a tracery vault with five artistically effective fields, which corresponded to the five high pyramids of the tent roof. The ribs of the vault are led into pillars built-in in the walls, the vault having no other means of support. No secular vaulted interior in Europe of that time could compete with the big Vladislav Hall. The large, three-part windows of the hall are the first manifestation of the Renaissance style in Bohemia. After the completion of the admired building Benedikt Ried was dubbed a knight in 1502.

The Ludvík Wing. After 1502 (up to 1510) B. Ried continued in the reconstruction of the Royal Palace by building a new transverse wing. The building was named after the successor to the throne, Ludvik, who was crowned as the Czech king in 1509 at the age of three.

Activity in the cathedral. Vladislav Jagiello, who spent a whole year at the Castle at that time, had St. Wenceslas's Chapel decorated with wall paintings and tried to secure the completion of St. Vitus's Cathedral. However, he only laid the foundations of the northern steeple, with which P. Parler's plan had probably not counted. Construction work was soon brought to a halt and only the torso of the structure remained, its building never being completed.

The portal of St. George's Basilica. The last work of B. Ried's workshop at Prague Castle was the southern portal of St. George's Basilica, a wholly Renaissance structure with a relief portraying St. George's battle with the dragon. It originated about 1515.

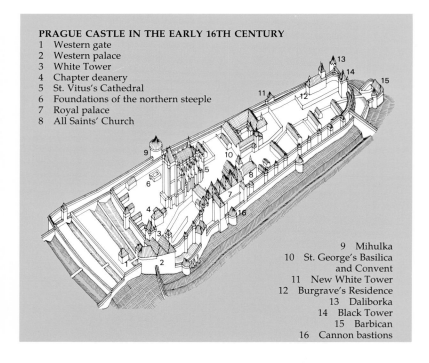

PRAGUE CASTLE IN THE EARLY 16TH CENTURY
1 Western gate
2 Western palace
3 White Tower
4 Chapter deanery
5 St. Vitus's Cathedral
6 Foundations of the northern steeple
7 Royal palace
8 All Saints' Church

9 Mihulka
10 St. George's Basilica and Convent
11 New White Tower
12 Burgrave's Residence
13 Daliborka
14 Black Tower
15 Barbican
16 Cannon bastions

1484	Vladislav Jagiello moves to Prague Castle, commencement of reconstruction
1490	Transfer of the permanent royal seat to Budapest
1493	Completion of the Royal Oratory in the cathedral
1502	Completion of the Vladislav Hall
1502–1510	Construction of the Ludvík Wing
1509	Painted decoration of St. Wenceslas's Chapel
	Founding of the northern steeple of the cathedral
c. 1515	Completion of the southern portal of St. George's Portal

The Castle During the Reign of the Hapsburgs in the 16th and 17th Centuries

The succession of the Hapsburgs. After the unfortunate death of the young King Ludvík in the Battle of Mainz the reign of the Jagiello dynasty came to an end. Ferdinand Hapsburg, consort of Anna, sister of Ludvík Jagiello, was elected king in St. Wenceslas's Chapel of St. Vitus's Cathedral. In the first phase of his reign he resided in Prague, but later he was represented here by the queen and the governor – Archduke Ferdinand Tyrol.

The Castle in the Renaissance period. With the transformation of the medieval castle into a Renaissance seat the king commenced the first adaptations of the residential interiors in the western part of the Royal Palace.

The founding of the Royal Garden. Ferdinand I began to build a garden, a typical part of Renaissance seats, in the northern foreground of the Castle. In order to secure access to it across the gorge of the River Brusnice he had a wooden bridge on five huge stone piers built at the same time. From 1538 a summer palace of exceptionally beautiful and valuable architecture began to originate on the eastern border of the garden, the king having summoned Italian artists to realize its construction.

A catastrophic fire. During the fire of 1541 the Little Quarter (Malá Strana), Prague Castle and the little town of Hradčany were severely damaged. The repair of the Castle was a lengthy and very costly procedure. It detained the progress of all the already commenced buildings, but at the same time it accelerated the penetration of the Renaissance style and afforded an opportunity for the construction of big palaces for the leading aristocratic Rožmberk and Pernštejn families at the Castle.

New building activity. In 1556 Bonifaz Wolmut became the royal architect. The outstanding buildings which he designed and realized include the upper floor and the roof of the Royal Summer Palace, the music choir in the cathedral, the top floor and the roof of St. Vitus's steeple, the vault of the Diet in the Royal Palace and the big Ball-games Hall in the Royal Garden. The Burgrave's Residence was rebuilt after a design by Giovanni Ventura and a central chapel consecrated to Adalbert and designed by Ulrico Avostalis originated in front of the western façade of St. Vitus's Cathedral.

Rudolph's Castle. The reign of Rudolph II gave rise to the all-round development of Prague Castle. The art-loving emperor, who resided permanently at the Castle, was a passionate builder and collector and a supporter of the sciences. His private chambers and studies were built in the western part of the southern wing of the Castle. He newly founded a northern wing, where he had two big halls (the present Spanish Hall and the Rudolph Gallery) built above the stables of his Spanish horses for his collections. These were also installed in the narrow communication wing forming the base of the present central wing between the First and the Third Courtyard. Rudolph had the gorge of the River Brusnice changed into an enclosure for deer and it is evident that this natural ditch has been called Stag Ditch since that time. He also had the masonry-built Lion Court, a pheasantry, a pond, an aviary and a summer riding-school built beyond the ditch.

The buildings of the Emperor Matyáš. When the Diet removed Rudolph II from the throne and installed his brother Matyáš on it Vienna once again became the imperial seat. Only two buildings at Prague Castle are connected with the name of the new sovereign: the pavilion in the southern gardens on the boundary of the Garden of Paradise (Rajská zahrada) and the garden called Na Valech (On the Ramparts) and particularly the western gate, traditionally referred to as the first Early Baroque structure in Prague.

A long period of wars. In 1618 the Catholic governors Jaroslav Bořita and Vilém Slavata of Chlum and with them the secretary Filip Fabricius were thrown from a window of the Czech Bureau in the Ludvík Wing. Their fall ended happily for them, but the event had tragic consequences for the country as a whole. The defenestration resulted in the unsuccessful uprising of the Estates and the outbreak of the Thirty Years' War. In the first half of the century Prague Castle was first occupied by Saxon and later Swedish troops. Destruction and looting were the consequence in both cases. The loss of a great part of the Rudolphian collections in particular is irreplaceable.

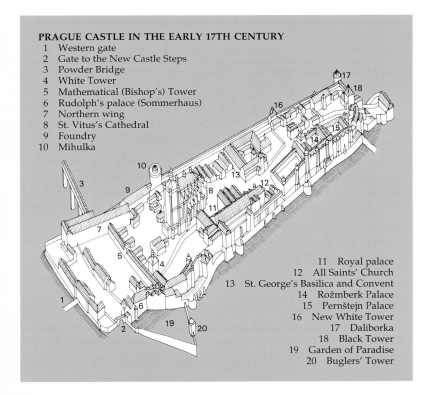

PRAGUE CASTLE IN THE EARLY 17TH CENTURY
 1   Western gate
 2   Gate to the New Castle Steps
 3   Powder Bridge
 4   White Tower
 5   Mathematical (Bishop's) Tower
 6   Rudolph's palace (Sommerhaus)
 7   Northern wing
 8   St. Vitus's Cathedral
 9   Foundry
10   Mihulka

11   Royal palace
12   All Saints' Church
13   St. George's Basilica and Convent
14   Rožmberk Palace
15   Pernštejn Palace
16   New White Tower
17   Daliborka
18   Black Tower
19   Garden of Paradise
20   Buglers' Tower

The "New Building" and the central wing. Although the period of wars was extremely unfavourable for the Castle, repairs and building works continued to be carried out. In the years 1638 to 1642 Giuseppe Mathei built the central part of the southern wing – the so-called New Building of the empress (Eleonara Gonzaga). During the next two years the central wing originated in its present extent as as residential quarters for the empress's entourage, the architect concerned being Dionysius Miseroni.

The cathedral and the basilica again. The Emperor Leopold I tried to secure the completion of the cathedral. He had the supporting pillars of the new nave of the cathedral founded, but soon afterwards brought the building work to a halt. However, in the early 17th century St. George's Convent was rebuilt. The basilica gained an Early Baroque façade.

During the sojourn of Leopold I in Prague. During the sojourn of the imperial court in Prague (1679–1680) the Castle became alive with ceremonies, balls and performances in a theatre converted from a ball-games hall. New fountains appeared in the Royal Garden and the Garden of Paradise. In the late 17th century a Riding-school designed by Jean Baptist Mathey originated in the foreground of the Castle.

1534	Founding of the Royal Garden
1535–1540	Construction of the Powder Bridge
1538	Commencement of the construction of the Royal Summer Palace
1541	Castle greatly damaged by fire
1548	The oldest building order of Prague Castle
1560–1563	Completion and roofing of the great steeple of St. Vitus's Cathedral
1567–1569	Construction of the Big Ball-games Hall
1575–1576	Construction of St. Adalbert's Chapel in front of the cathedral
1580	Completion of the repairs of Old Saints' Church
1583	Transfer of the seat of the Emperor Rudolph II to Prague Castle
1589	Completion of the royal mausoleum and the royal graves in the cathedral
1590	Construction of the structure for fig trees
1597–1598	Construction of the Rudolph Gallery
1602–1606	Construction of the Spanish Hall
1612	Transfer of the seat of the Emperor Matyáš to Vienna
1618	Defenestration of the governors
1631	Occupation of the Castle by Saxon troops
1648	Occupation of the Castle by Swedish troops, looting of the art collections
1673	Commencement of the completion of St. Vitus's Cathedral by the Emperor Leopold I
1694–1695	Construction of the Riding-school

The Castle During the Reign of the Hapsburgs in the 18th and 19th Centuries

The adaptation of the Castle for the coronation. In the first half of the 18th century Prague Castle was the scene of two big and ostentatious ceremonies: the coronation of the Emperor Charles VI as Czech king and the sanctification of John Nepomuk. In the course of the preparations for the coronation (1723) the residential interiors in the central and southern wings as well as several rooms in the Royal Palace were restyled. A kitchen was built by the Building Bureau and another two big stables were erected in the neighbourhood of the Big Ball-games Hall (already converted into a stable). An open-air theatre was built on the area of the summer riding-school, the opera composed for the coronation ceremonies being performed in it under the baton of the court conductor J. J. Fuchs.

The St. John ceremonies. The preparations for the sanctification of John Nepomuk were also realized on a grand scale. The years 1718 to 1722 had already seen the growth of a chapel consecrated to this patron saint of the Czech Kingdom in St. George's Basilica. However, the sanctification took place in 1729. The festivities, in which an enormous number of people took part, lasted a whole week. In the following years (1733–1736) St. John Nepomuk's silver tombstone was made in Vienna for St. Vitus's Cathedral.

The Theresian reconstruction. The last general reconstruction of Prague Castle is connected with the name of the Empress Maria Theresa. The beginning of her reign was marked by wars over the Hapsburg heritage. In 1741 Prague was occupied by French and Saxon allied troops and in 1744 by the Prussian army. Great damage was done to the Castle by gun-fire during the next Prussian siege in 1757. Three years earlier the empress had laid the foundation stone for the converting of what was originally Rožmberk Palace into the Institute of Gentlewomen after a plan by Nicola Pacassi. He was entrusted with another, even more important order: the reconstruction of all the wings of the so-called New Palace of Prague Castle.

Unified façades. The result of the reconstruction was to be the transformation of the still medieval Castle into a representative seat of the château type. Building works proceeded successively from 1755 to 1775 under the supervision of the architects Anselmo Luragho, Antonín Kuntz and Antonín Haffenecker. The height of all the wings was unified and their façades were also lent the same appearance. A cour d'honneur (the First Courtyard) was built on the western side of the Castle and a new chapel consecrated to the Holy Rood originated on the site of the coronation kitchen and the Building Bureau. The Theresian Wing, built from 1766 to 1768, served to connect the Old Royal Palace with the Institute of Gentlewomen. The appearance of the Castle from the north also changed: the bridge spanning Stag Ditch was replaced with a huge embankment under which the original bridge piers disappeared.

Troops in valuable buildings. The reign of Joseph II brought the Castle many unfortunate events. The Big Ball-games Hall, the Royal Summer Palace, the Riding-school and St. George's Convent were placed by the emperor at the disposal of troops, who for long years greatly damaged them due to their unsuitable conduct. In 1782 everything that remained of the renowned Rudolphian collections was scattered as the result of auction sales.

The Emperor Ferdinand V's dower house. The importance of Prague Castle as the centre of the Czech Kingdom continued to decline in the following century. In 1848 the Emperor Ferdinand, called the Benign, made it his permanent seat after his abdication, having the Chapel of the Holy Rood in the Second Courtyard newly adapted for his small court. During the preparations of the coronation of his nephew Franz Joseph I as Czech king the Spanish Hall and the Rudolph Gallery were newly decorated. (However, neither this nor any other coronation took place at Prague Castle.)

The completion of St. Vitus's Cathedral. In the latter half of the 19th century the Castle witnessed a grand building event in the form of the completion of St. Vitus's Cathedral. On this occasion, however, the initiator was not the sovereign, but the Union for the Completion of the Cathedral. It began its activity in 1859 and under the successive supervision of the architects Josef Kranner, Josef Mocker and Kamil Hilbert it succeeded in having the medieval part repaired and secured and the cathedral wholly architecturally completed by 1929.

The New Deanery. A new chapter deanery and two cannons' residences in the square U svatého Jiří also originated after a project by Josef Mocker.

St. George's Basilica. At the turn of the 19th and 20th centuries St. George's Basilica not only underwent necessary architectural repairs, but also its reconstruction into its "original" Romanesque form in the spirit of the puristic principles of the time.

1725	Commencement of Baroque adaptations of the Royal Garden
1736	Completion of the silver tombstone of St. John Nepomuk
1741	Occupation of the Castle by French troops
1754	Commencement of construction of the Institute of Gentlewomen
1755–1775	Reconstruction of the Castle
1757	Castle damaged by artillery fire during the Prussian siege
1764	Consecration of the new chapel consecrated to the Holy Rood
1766–1768	Construction of the Theresian Wing
1844–1846	Conversion of the Royal Summer Palace into a picture gallery
1865–1868	The Spanish Hall and the Rudolph Gallery adapted and provided with new decoration
1861–1873	Repair of the old part of St. Vitus's Cathedral by the Union for the Completion of the Cathedral
1873	Laying of the foundation stone for the completion of the cathedral
1878–1880	Construction of the New Deanery

Prague Castle the Seat of the President

The state centre of the Republic. After the origin of the Czechoslovak Republic in 1918 Prague Castle once again became the state centre in the full extent. However, without undergoing repair the neglected buildings could not serve for either state representation or as the seat and work place of the head of state. The most urgent tasks were taken on by the architect Kamil Hilbert and in 1920 by the architect Josip Plečnik, a Slovenian living in Prague.

J. Plečnik's modifications of the southern gardens. The first task of the new architect lay in the modification of the southern gardens – the Garden of Paradise and the Garden on the Ramparts. His plan had a clear and relatively simple conception. He enriched the connected gardens with observation points, pavilions and small structures characterized by a refined shape and careful craft work. Later he lent a new, individual character to the Garden on the Bastion (Zahrada Na Baště).

The First Courtyard. J. Plečnik's idea of the First Courtyard was only partly realized. Granite paving, flag poles and lighting originated after his designs, but the closing of the Matthias Gate, whose function was to be taken over by new passageways, and the placing of the state emblem in front of the gate after Plečnik's ideas did not come about.

The Third Courtyard. The reconstruction of the Third Courtyard had a strong influence on the results of the archeological research carried out here from 1925. A considerable part of the Third Courtyard now rests on a reinforced concrete panel covering the area of the archeological excavations. The appearance of the courtyard changed after it had been levelled to one elevation, its new dominant being a monolith of Mrákotín granite. The bronze statue of St. George was transferred from the Early Baroque foundation to a simple diorite pedestal with a bronze balustrade. The Third Courtyard was connected with the Garden on the Ramparts by the Bulls' Staircase, named after the bronze bulls bearing the original roofing of the entrance.

The living quarters of President Masaryk. J. Plečnik's most important task in the interior of the Castle was the construction of living quarters for the president of the Republic on the second floor of the southern and central wings. (The reception rooms on the first floor mainly kept their appearance of the 18th and 19th centuries). Plečnik originally also designed the approach to the president's quarters: from the passageway reserved for the president's carriage or car via a spiral staircase or a cylindrical lift situated on its hollow spindle.

The tasks of other architects. J. Plečnik's work was separately followed up by his close co-worker Otto Rothmayer, who reconstructed the area in front of the Spanish Hall – now called

Rothmayer's Hall – and the Wedge Passage. In 1952 he completed his remarkable reconstruction of the Theresian Wing, begun before the war. J. Plečnik was replaced in his function as court architect by Pavel Janák in 1936. His main task was the reconstruction of important buildings in the foreground of the Castle – the Riding-school, the Big Ball-games Hall and the Royal Summer Palace.

National Monument No. 1. A law of 1958 proclaimed the Castle National Cultural Monument No. 1. Moreover, it has always been under the constant even if superficial control of the public, also being a grand representative of state for foreign visits. For this reason great attention was devoted to its maintenance and restoration even when general care for historic monuments was more than inadequate.

Good and bad reconstructions. The post-war repairs of the Castle were mainly of a reconstruction character, but the approach to them varied. The Picture Gallery of Prague Castle, newly opened in 1964, is an example of the sensitive adaptation of a historic interior. The adaptation of St. George's Convent for the needs of the National Gallery, completed in 1976, resulted, on the contrary, in marked changes in the character of its interior, which were fortunately not manifested externally. When the Burgrave's Residence was converted into the House of Czechoslovak Children in the Sixties its historic parts were even demolished and replaced with a modern annex. The adaptation of the entrance to the Spanish Hall of 1973 to 1975 also evokes negative response nowadays. Fortunately, other mainly politically motivated proposals were not realized even at that time: for example, the replacement of Mocker's houses in the square U svatého Jiří with new, modern buildings, the founding of an

MOSAIC PORTRAYING THE BIG EMBLEM OF THE CZECHOSLOVAK REPUBLIC

Avenue of Socialism, the establishment of a Monument of the History of the Czechoslovak People in St. George's Convent, or a Museum of Work in Lobkowicz Palace.

The purpose of reconstructions. The preservation of monuments for the future, their adaptation for the purpose of new use with minimum disturbance of their historic essence – such were the aims of the reconstructions, most of which also fulfilled them. The following monuments were opened after undergoing reconstruction: the Powder Tower – Mihulka (1982), Lobkowicz Palace (1987), the Royal Summer Palace (1990), Daliborka 1990, the Foundry (1990), the Imperial Stable and the Foundry Court (1993) and the Theresian Wing (1993). The graffito decoration of the Big Ball-games Hall, the reliefs of the Royal Summer Palace and the plaster work in the Spanish Hall, various parts of the inner furnishings, altars, the articles of the St. Vitus treasure, furniture, gobelins and paintings have been restored.

The gardens of Prague Castle. The Royal Garden, accessible only exceptionally during the First Republic and practically permanently closed after the building of the presidential residence (1947–1949), was opened permanently to the public in March 1990. A part of the reconstructed southern gardens was made accessible again in 1991, the remaining part being opened after the completion of all the reconstruction works in 1993.

1918	Prague Castle the seat of the president of the Czechoslovak Republic
1920	Commencement of adaptations of the Castle by architect J. Plečnik
1925	Commencement of systematic archeological research
1921–1924	Adaptations of the southern gardens
1922–1923	Adaptations of the First Courtyard
1923–1924	Adaptations of the presidential residential quarters
1924–1929	Adaptations of the Third Courtyard
1927	Adaptations of the Hall of Columns in the western wing
1927–1929	Construction of the Bulls' Staircase
1929	End of the completion of St. Vitus's Cathedral
1930	Adaptation of the Garden on the Bastion
1945	Occurrence of fire in the Big Ball-games Hall
1947–1949	Construction of a presidential dwelling-house in the Royal Garden
1949	Completion of the reconstruction of the Riding-school
1952	Completion of the reconstruction of the Big Ball-games Hall and the Theresian Wing
1954	Completion of the reconstruction of the Royal Summer Palace
1964	Completion of the reconstruction of the Picture Gallery of Prague Castle
1965	Commencement of the gradual repair of the outer mantle of St. Vitus's Cathedral
1976	Completion of the reconstruction of St. George's Convent
1987	Completion of the reconstruction of Lobkowicz Palace
1990	Completion of the reconstruction of the southern wing and the reception rooms
1993	Completion of the reconstruction of the southern gardens Commencement of the reconstruction of the Third Courtyard

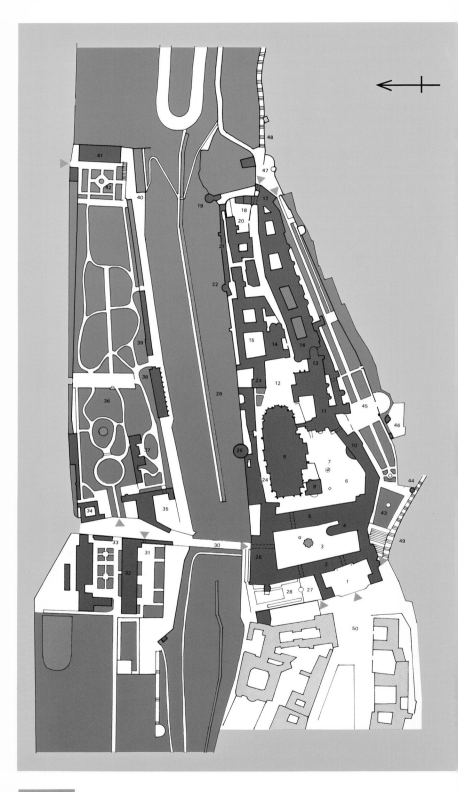

PLAN OF PRAGUE CASTLE

A SIGHTSEEING TOUR OF THE CASTLE

THE ENTRANCE AREA OF THE CASTLE AND THE CASTLE COURTYARDS

Hradčanské Square

Hradčanské Square (a part of the originally pagan and, from the late 16th century, the royal town of Hradčany) is a dignified area affording access to the Castle.

Its shorter, western side oposite the Castle is closed by the symmetrical façade of Tuscany Palace, whose Early Baroque architecture with an inner courtyard is the work of G. B. Mathey of the late 17th century.

The longer, northern side of the square is formed in the direction towards the Castle by a part of Martinic Palace with a Late Renaissance façade remaining from the reconstruction of Jaroslav Bořita of Martinic, several large Baroque houses, some with the metropolitan emblem of St. Vitus's chapter, and the Archbishop's Palace. This large, in essence Renaissance building has undergone several reconstructions. Its present façade with rich Rococo decoration originated in 1764 to 1765

after a design by J. Virch. At the same time it was decorated with statues Faith and Hope by T. Seidan. By passing through a passageway we come to Šternberk Palace, which was situated lower down the slope and was wholly concealed in a view from the square. It is outstanding not only for its Baroque architecture – realized after a project by D. Martinelli of the turn of the 17th and 18th centuries – but nowadays also for the permanent expositions of Old European Art from the collections of the National Gallery installed in it.

On the southern side of the square, in the direction away from the Castle, stands Salmovský Palace, converted from older buildings in the first decade of the 19th century, and Schwarzenberg Palace, built about the mid-16th century at the time of John the Younger of Luxembourg. This palace in particular arouses attention due to its rich Renaissance architecture and graffito decoration, renovated too conspicuously, however. Adjoining Schwarzenberg Palace is the Convent of the mendicant Carmelites with St. Benedict's Church. It has often been incorrectly

referred to as the convent of the Barnabites, most likely because it originally belonged to the male Barnabite order. In 1792, however, they left the convent to make way for the Carmelite nuns from the abolished convent in the Little Quarter.

On the green area in the centre of the square stands a statue of Our Lady surrounded by statues of eight saints. The sculptures are the work of the well-known Prague sculptor F. M. Brokoff. The column on which the statue of Our Lady stands was raised as an expression of thanks for the end of the plague in 1726.

During World War II remainders of the masonry of a Romanesque house were discovered in the course of the hollowing-out of a fire reservoir on the boundary of the small park nearer the Castle. This important find documenting the settlement of the foreground of the Castle was saved, secretly transferred below the ground level of the Third Courtyard of the Castle by policemen and regrouped in its original form.

The main entrance to Prague Castle runs from Hradčanské Square to the First Courtyard.

The First Courtyard

The western entrance to the Castle was always the most important one and so exceptional attention was devoted to its fortification. The Castle was originally separated from Hradčany Square of the present by a natural gorge – the Hradčany Furrow, converted into a deep ditch in the Middle Ages. During the reign of Vladislav Jagiello (1471–1516) it was joined by two other ditches. Bridges spanning these ditches afforded access to the Castle.

The two inner ditches were filled-in in the late 16th century, the outer, third ditch ceasing to exist during the Theresian reconstruction in the 18th century, when the western side of the Castle gained the form of a cour d'honneur. It was only then that the First Courtyard originated. It owes its last, present appearance to the court architect J. Plečnik and is dated after 1920.

We enter the First Courtyard by passing through a gate with the monograms of Marie Theresa and Joseph II. A row of pillars bears a monumental group of statues of battling giants and a smaller couple of putti with vases or with the symbols of the Czech kingdom (a

GATE TO THE FIRST COURTYARD

lion) and the Hapsburg monarchy (an eagle). They are the work of the sculptor I. F. Platzer the Elder of 1770 to 1771. In 1921 the originals were replaced with copies sculptured by A. Procházka and Č. Vosmík.

The paving, lighting and flagpoles (originally of fir trunks, but in 1962 exchanged for poles stuck together from separate parts) originated after a design by J. Plečnik at the beginning of the First Republic.

The Castle wing closing the First Courtyard was built with the use of some older walls after a project by N. Pacassi in 1763 to 1771 and decorated on its attics with statues and military trophies by I. F. Platzer the Elder.

Entrance to the western wing is gained by passing through the Matthias Gate, traditionally designated the first Baroque structure in Prague. It was named after the Emperor Matthias, whose titles it bears along with the date 1614. However, due to the fact that the inscription is executed in plaster, while the gate as a whole is of sandstone, the impression arises that this monument originated at an ear-

lier date. Its design is attributed to G. M. Filippi, one of the leading architects working in Prague already during the reign of Rudolph II.

CASTLE GUARD

CEREMONIAL STAIRCASE
FROM THE MATTHIAS GATE

Behind the Matthias Gate a ceremonial staircase runs from the inner space with Rococo stucco work on the right to the reception rooms on the first floor. It is the work of N. Pacassi and I. F. Platzer and occupies the site of an older staircase leading to the private chambers of Rudolph II.

On the left side it is possible to take a look at the monumental hall of columns named after the architect J. Plečnik. This interior is one of the most important of Plečnik's works at Prague Castle. It originated from 1927 to 1931, the staircase being added in 1975 during the adaptations of the entrance to the Spanish Hall.
Nowadays the northern and southern wings are used for the accommodation of state visitors, the western tract serving representative purposes.

The Second Courtyard

The Second Courtyard originated on the area of the former western outer bailey. One whole half of its present area was taken up by a huge ditch in front of a Romanesque fortification wall, still preserved in the present central wing between the Second and Third Courtyards.

It was not until the latter half of the 16th century that the ditch was filled-in and a narrow connecting tract built along the wall in which Rudolph II installed his collections. The original Bishop's Gate of the Middle Ages was enclosed in this tract, a staircase connecting the individual floors and leading to an observation terrace.
Similarly, the huge Romanesque White Tower, originally serving for the protection of the western entrance, is built-in in the present western wing, built on the site of chapter houses as late as the 17th century. In the Middle Ages it became a prison in which, among others, Prince Soběslav II, Záviš of Falkenštejn and King Václav IV were imprisoned. It was Rudolph II who finally transferred the prison from here to the so-called New White Tower near the Golden Lane (Zlatá ulička).
Projecting from the central wing into the courtyard is the Chapel of the Holy Rood. Its building history is relatively variegated: in the 16th century its site was occupied by the building of the Court Building Bureau, enlarged in the 18th century by a kitchen for the coronation of Charles VI (1723). The present chapel

ENTRANCE TO THE SECOND COURTYARD

SECOND COURTYARD

INTERIOR OF THE CHAPEL
OF THE HOLY ROOD

was built by A. Luragho after a project by Pacassi during the Theresian reconstruction of 1758 to 1763. Preserved in particular of its original furnishings are the marble high altar with sculptures of angels by I. F. Platzer the Elder and a painting The Crucifixion by F. X. Balko and other paintings by F. X. Balko on the side altars: St. Wenceslas with St. Vitus and St. Theresa with St. Francis. The rest of the decoration dates in the years 1852 to 1856, when the chapel was adapted for the ex-Emperor Ferdinand, who resided at Prague Castle after his abdication. The ceiling paintings with scenes from the Old Testament and murals (scenes from the New Testament, the figures of prophets and church fathers) are attributed to V. Kandler and the statue of St. John Nepomuk to E. Max. The sculptures of SS. Peter and Paul in niches on the outer side of the east end are also his work (In the years 1961 to 1990 a part of the St. Vitus Treasure was exhibited in the interior of the Chapel of the Holy Rood.)

Concealed in the passageway to the south of the Chapel of the Holy Rood is a tower-shaped gate from the Jagiello period: the main (western) entrance to the inner Castle was situated here from the beginning.

Since Plečnik's adaptations the gateway has served as the <u>private entrance to the living quarters and study of the president.</u>

The narrower part of the courtyard is closed by a <u>short sector of the southern wing,</u> built in its core in the late 15th century by B. Ried as a separate palace on the foundations of a Romanesque wall. After the fire of 1541 the palace was rebuilt as the so-called New Building of the Archduke Ferdinand Tyrol and later connected with other separately standing buildings further to the west. The Emperor Rudolph II had this part newly reconstructed and raised in height and it was just here that he established his private chambers (the so-called Sommerhaus) on the upper floors.

<u>The long façade of the western wing originated during the Theresian adaptations</u> on the site of older buildings. Originally situated here were the former houses of the metropolitan chapter and, from the 16th century, the big house of the Supreme Chamberlain. However, the oldest building here was a church, at the same time the first masonry building at the Castle. It was consecrated to Our Lady and founded by Prince Bořivoj at the end of the 9th century. Its masonry was discovered here in 1952 by the archeologist I. Borkovský.

<u>In the northern wing there are long vaulted Renaissance stables along both sides of the passageway from Powder Bridge.</u> Stables stood here already at Ferdinand I's time, but the preserved quarters were built in the late 16th century by Rudolph II for his Spanish horses. This influenced the later naming of the Spanish Hall, built in the early 17th century along with the Rudolph Gallery above the stables.) All three interiors of the stables have been newly adapted for exhibition purposes: the two in parallel on the western side of the passageway as a part of the Picture Gallery of the Castle and the one on the eastern side as a separate exhibition hall.

<u>The Early Baroque Fountain in the Second Courtyard – the work of the stonemason Francesco de Torre and the sculptor Jeroným Kohl of 1686</u>

KOHL'S FOUNTAIN AND WELL IN THE SECOND COURTYARD

– was hewn from rough Žehrovice sandstone, which was a popular material in the Baroque period. The lower bowl of the fountain in the shape of a four-leafed clover rests on three steps. The rounded part is decorated with festoons with fruit and cartouches in which, below the imperial crown, is the gilded initial L (the Emperor Leopold I 1657–1705). Standing on the cornice of the central pillar are four statues of classical gods supporting a stone bowl. They are: Hercules dressed in a lion's skin, Neptune with a dolphin, Vulcan with a hammer and anvil and Mercury with small wings at his ankles and on his helmet. On the bowl, from which water runs through four holes in masks, there are two figures of Tritons with fish tails. These bear the upper bowl. The summit of the fountain is formed by three lions spurting water from their jaws. As old engravings show us, the painted Austrian two-headed eagle, cut out from tin plate, was originally set in a stone sphere on their heads. This was evidently removed during the First Republic and placed in the depository of Prague Castle.

<u>The well,</u> whose depth is 14 metres, evidently dates in the 16th century. Its present cover was allegedly made in 1719. An iron grille with a dense wire network rests on its profiled sandstone edge. In its lower part it adapted to the old, now disassembled pumping equipment. It terminates at the top with a rich stylized flower.

The present paving of the Second Courtyard originated after a design by J. Fragner in 1965 to 1967. Near the east end of the Chapel of the Holy Rood there also used to stand a granite fountain likewise designed by J. Fragner and decorated with a statue of a lion by V. Makovský. In 1986 it was damaged by a vehicle and never renewed. The heavily damaged statue was restored and placed in the depository.

At present the interiors on the level of the first floor of each wing serve reception purposes, while those on the second and third floors of the central sing are used by the Office of the President of the Czech Republic.

The Third Courtyard

The irregular area of the biggest of the Castle courtyards is demarcated by the central and southern wings of the Castle, the western façade of the Old Royal Palace and the southern side of St. Vitus's Cathedral.

In the Early Middle Ages the naturally sloping terrain was built-up with small wooden houses. On the highest

VIEW FROM ST. VITUS'S STEEPLE

THIRD COURTYARD WITH THE OLD DEANERY AND THE CATHEDRAL

elevation of the rocky ridge (the environs of the Old Deanery and St. Vitus's Cathedral) the level of the ground was markedly higher than it is today. The slope was gradually levelled and in the 14th century, when the area became a courtyard, it was arranged into two elevations separated by a supporting wall.

In the Baroque period the courtyard was decorated with a large fountain below the statue of St. George. At first it stood by the southern wing, but later it was transferred to the supporting wall.

Already from 1920 old masonry was unearthed during excavations on the

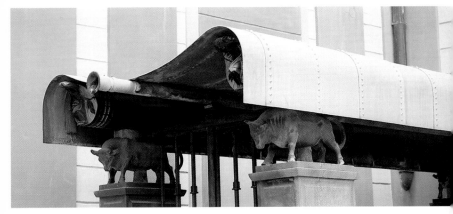

BULLS' STAIRCASE

area of the courtyard and so in 1925 extensive <u>archeological research</u> was started. In view of the importance of

STATUE OF ST. GEORGE
IN FRONT OF THE OLD DEANERY

its results the unearthed masonry and remainders of wooden structures and mounds were not newly concealed, but <u>covered with a reinforced concrete structure.</u> This task was fulfilled by the architect J. Plečnik. He had the paving, broken up by diagonal bands, built of large granite panels and at the same time he levelled the courtyard to one elevation. The new <u>dominant feature of the courtyard</u>, a <u>slender pylon made of a single piece of Mrákotín granite,</u> is also J. Plečnik's work. It was raised in 1928 as a memorial to the victims of World War I. (Originally it was to have been terminated with an allegorical statue, the circular area below the foundations of the monolith being intended for the grave of an unkown warrior.) The <u>roofing</u> of the older excavations near the cathedral and the modifications of the statue of St. George and the Eagle Fountain in front of the Old Royal Palace were realized <u>after designs</u> by J. Plečnik similarly as the so-called <u>Bulls' Staircase</u> leading to the Garden on the Ramparts. Thus the present appearance of the courtyard is the result of modifications designed down to the last detail by the first Castle architect in the independent Republic.

The realization of these modifications came to end in 1929, when the millennium of St. Wenceslas was celebrated. Insulation was not provided under the paving by the fixed date, perhaps due to a lack of time. After the elapse of several years water penetrated into the area of the excavations and threatened to

damage the structure proper. For this reason an essential extensive reconstruction of the courtyard was started in 1993.

The Fourth Courtyard

The Fourth Courtyard is the name of the area to which access is gained through a grille-type gate from the corner of Hradčanské Square, from the Archbishop's Palace. However, it is not a courtyard in the real sense of the word, but rather a small yard whose outer side adjoins the northern promontory and a part of the western wing of the Castle. It joins up with the somewhat higher situated Garden on the Bastion, which in 1930 the architect J. Plečnik adapted in the style of southern and Japanese gardens.

The name On the Bastion brings the older medieval fortifications here to mind. The ground was definitely levelled as late as during the Theresian reconstruction of the Castle and its first park-like arrangement in front of the outer entrance to the Spanish Hall originated in 1861.

Through a passageway it is possible to pass from the Fourth Courtyard to the Second Castle Courtyard, or by walking through the Garden on the Bastion pass round the north-western part of the Castle to its northern entrance from the street U Prašného mostu.

EAGLE FOUNTAIN

FOURTH COURTYARD

WESTERN FAÇADE OF CATHEDRAL

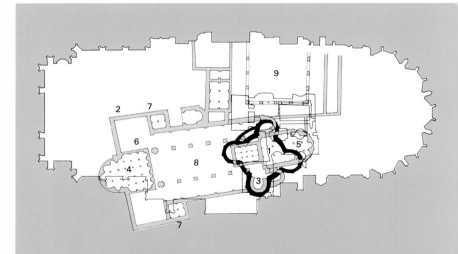

OLDER CHURCHES CONSECRATED TO ST. VITUS

1 St. Vitus's Rotunda
2 Basilica of SS. Vitus,
   Wenceslas and Adalbert
3 St. Wenceslav's grave
4 Western choir

5 Eastern choir
6 Transverse nave
7 Steeples
8 Triple nave
9 Monastery of the Church of Prague

ST. VITUS'S CATHEDRAL

Its Architectural Development

By walking through the passageway in the central wing we pass from the Second to the Third Courtyard and directly to the western façade of the cathedral. St. Vitus's Cathedral is the biggest of all Prague's churches and it is the third building built on the same site. About 925 Prince Václav founded a rotunda with four apses which in 1061 made way for a more spacious, triple-naved basilica with two choirs and two steeples. In the latter half of the 11th century the basilica was completed and in the 13th century it was rebuilt and enlarged. This second church consecrated to St. Vitus was later gradually demolished with the continuing construction of the cathedral, founded in 1344.

Its first builder, Matthias of Arras, succeeded in completing the polygonal choir chapel and gallery before his death in 1352.

After a short period, during which building works were not brought to a halt, the supervision of the construction activity was taken over by the young Peter Parler, who completed the choir and closed its vault (1385) and built St. Wenceslas's Chapel, the Golden Portal and the lower part of the main steeple.

After his death, from 1399, the building was continued by his sons John and Wenceslas until the beginning of the Hussite wars.

From then on the cathedral remained unfinished for whole centuries in spite of two attempts to continue in its construction: Vladislav Jagiello had the foundations of the northern steeple laid in the years 1509 to 1511 and in 1673 Leopold I had the pillars of the Baroque triple nave built. At the end of the 15th century, however, the Royal Oratory was built in the cathedral (H. Spiess, B. Ried) and in the Renaissance period the main steeple was completed and the music choir built (B. Wolmut). A remarkable manneristic building in the form of the central chapel consecrated to St. Adalbert (O. Avostalis) was built in front of the provisional western façade of the cathedral, being demolished during the completion work in the 19th century. The Baroque period was marked in particular by the addition of interior features, the most outstanding of which is the tombstone of St. John Nepomuk.

Under the leadership of J. Kranner the Union for the Completion of St. Vitus's Cathedral, founded in 1859, first repaired the medieval part. Afterwards – from 1873 – the cathedral was completed – after a project by J. Mocker, who headed the building work until his death in 1899. His continuator K. Hilbert realized changes in a few parts and headed the whole work to the finish, to the St. Wenceslas millennium (1929).

CENTRAL PORTAL

ST. VITUS'S CATHEDRAL

Exterior

The western façade of the cathedral. When viewed from the west the cathedral impresses the viewer with its height, which of necessity has to be observed at too close a distance. It outwardly betrays the basic ground-plan of the cathedral: the gable wall of the main nave is closed from the sides by the steeples closing the side aisles. The row of side chapels is not manifested in the façade.

The entrance portals. Conspicuous horizontal elements divide the western wall into three parts of different heights. The lower part, below the tracery balustrade of the gallery, is articulated by three

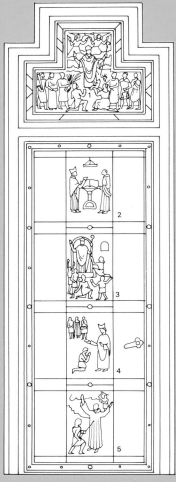

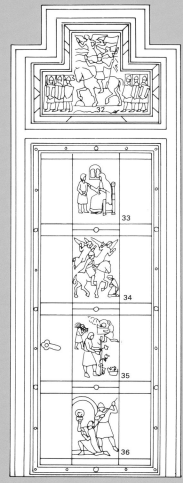

LEFT DOOR   RIGHT DOOR

RELIEFS OF BRONZE DOORS
1 St. Adalbert blessing the nation
2 Education of St. Adalbert in Magdeburg
3 St. Adalbert saving Vršovec's wife
4 St. Adalbert baptising the Hungarian king St. Stephen
5 The death of St. Adalbert
6 St. Wenceslas receiving relics of St. Vitus from the hands of the Emperor Jindřich
7 The founding of St. Vitus's Rotunda
8 The consecration of the rotunda and the transfer of relics
9 Spytihněv II founding the basilica
10 The consecration of the basilica
11 Charles IV handing over the remains of St. Vitus to Archbishop Arnošt of Pardubice
12 Charles IV with his son Václav in Peter Parler's workshop
13 Matthias of Arras on the building of the cathedral
14 Václav Michal Pešina founding the new part of the cathedral
15 The consecration of the completed building
16 Spytihněv II
17 Vratislav II
18 Charles IV

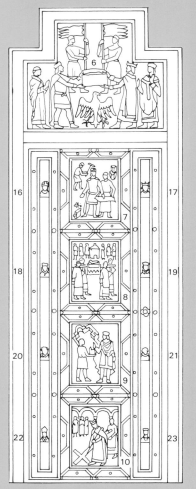
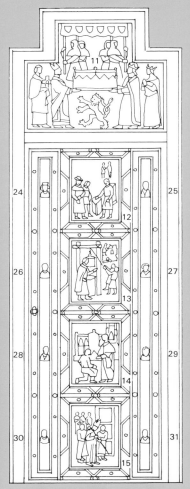

CENTRAL DOOR

entrance portals. All of them – richly articulated and decorated – are of the same design: they all have their own entrance with a bronze relief door and a figural tympanum in a broken arch. And they are all terminated with a steep, triangular gable with blind tracery. The central portal leads below the western choir to the main nave, while the two side portals lead to the interiors below the steeples. The reliefs of the bronze doors are the work of O. Španiel of 1927 to 1929 and were realized after a design by the painter V. H. Brunner. The northern portal is devoted to St. Adalbert and the southern one to the legend about St. Wenceslas. The doors of the double entrance in the centre are decorated with scenes from the history of the building of the cathedral. The sandstone tympana with reliefs The Nativity, Crucifixion and Ascension of the Lord were carved out by J. Žák after designs by K. Dvořák and L. Piša. They were gradually set in place in 1553, 1956 and 1965.

GARGOYLES ABOVE THE NEW PART OF THE CATHEDRAL

BELL CALLED ZIKMUND (18 TONS)

The round window. The upper part of the façade is dominated by an enormous round window (diameter 10.40 m), set in a broken arch. Set in a gusset below the window are double portraits of the builders of the cathedral of the time of the completion of the cathedral. They are the work of V. Sucharda of 1929. On the right the sculptor portrayed J. Mocker and K. Hilbert and on the left J. Wirth and F. Kysela.

The statues on the façade. Below the baldachin on the supporting pillars of the steeple there are statues of Charles IV, the work of S. Sucharda of 1903, and Arnošt of Pardubice, sculpted by L. Kofránek in 1952, on the sides of the rosette. Above them, in recesses on consoles, there are fourteen statues of saints representing the work of various artists of 1903. (Only a small part of the original idea of decorating the western portal and the façade of the steeple with forty-six sculptures was thus realized.)

The highest part is separated by a band of blind traceries. In the sector between the steeples the medieval tracery on the southern façade of the side nave is literally repeated. The gable is also covered with rich tracery, the two western steeples terminating with broken stone pyramids.

The southern façade. The whole southern façade can be seen well from the Third Courtyard. The original Gothic part is clearly separated from the later Neo-Gothic part by a great tower. The difference in the colour of the sandstone is still very marked.

The great (southern) steeple. Apart from two remarkable consoles above the gallery with motifs of legendary animals, recognizable also from ground level, the façade of the steeple has a particularly conspicuous feature in the form of a pointed window. Its rich, ornamental and

GRILLE IN THE WINDOW
OF THE GREAT STEEPLE

gilded grille and tablet with a crowned R date from the time of Rudolph II. Hanging behind it is St. Vitus's biggest bell, called Zikmund. The steeple terminates with an observation gallery and a helmet with copper roofing and four corner turrets.

In the upper part of the the steeple there are two unusual dials, each of which has one hand only. The upper dial, set in the window tracery, shows the hours, the lower one indicating the ouarters of an hour and the minutes between them. Both belong to a single clockwork dating in the late 16th century and situated on the top floor of the steeple.

The Golden Portal. The so-called Golden Portal, situated next to the great steeple, is the solemn entrance to the cathedral. Its three pointed arches open on to a vestibule roofed with a saddle vault. The articulation of the walls, consoles and baldachins (prepared for unrealized sculptural decoration) have all been very precisely reconstructed according to fragments found at the time of the completion of the building.

The façade above the entrance arches is decorated with a mosaic picture The Last Judgement, with a group of Czech patron saints in the centre and with the kneeling figures of Charles IV and his consort Eliška Pomořanská below.

Only the console with oak leaves on the central pillar between the door and the vault consoles on the two opposite pillars with motifs of the legendary bird Phoenix and a pelican feeding its young with its own blood is originally Gothic. The two mosaic portraits realized after designs by K. Svolinský (Adam and Eve, The Crucifixion) are modern works. The interior of the vestibule is closed in the direction of the courtyard by

COMMEMORATIVE INSCRIPTION (1396)

a grille with bronze reliefs of the calendarium and the signs of the Zodiac by J. Horejc (1955) and in the direction of the cathedral by a door designed by J. Sokol (1964).

There is a small window with a grille on the area of the mosaic which leads to the crown chamber, where the coronation jewels of the Czech kings are kept.

The pointed arch at the head of the transverse nave above the Golden Portal is filled with Neo-Gothic tracery with the St. Wenceslas crown on its top. It brings lace to mind and is original Gothic in style.

The spiral staircase. On the right side of the façade of the transverse nave there is a remarkable southern spiral staircase, unquestionably hewn by Peter Parler himself. A person ascending it changes the direction of winding three times. Another masterly work is the airy, broken mantle of the staircase on which the provincial emblems are composed.

The choir part of the cathedral. The Gothic part of the choir with a ring of choir chapels continues from the Golden Portal in easterly direction. Apart from a few details, the design of the chapels and the form of the outer supporting system are repeated.

GOLDEN PORTAL

OUTER SUPPORTING SYSTEM
OF THE OLD PART

Built-in between the buttresses of St. John Nepomuk's Chapel on the south-eastern side of the choir is the saint's sandstone cenotaph – the work of J. F. Platzer of 1763.

ST. VITUS'S CATHEDRAL
Interior

The division of the cathedral
A breath-taking view of the interior of the cathedral opens up behind the entrance portal of the western façade. As the completion of the cathedral was perfectly adapted to the style of the medieval part, the whole interior merges to form a unified environment at first sight. The centre of the cathedral is formed by the main nave with a high vault and a high choir joining up with it. The area is richly illuminated by big windows taking up the whole area of the wall from one supporting pillar to another. The main nave is lined with narrower side aisles. Both are lined in turn with a continuous row of side chapels opening on to the cathedral. Corresponding to them in the choir part is a gallery with a ring of choir chapels. The transverse nave forms an imaginary cross in the ground-plan of the cathedral.

INTERIOR OF THE CATHEDRAL
(total length 124 m, height of vault 33 m, height of steeple 96.5 m) ▶

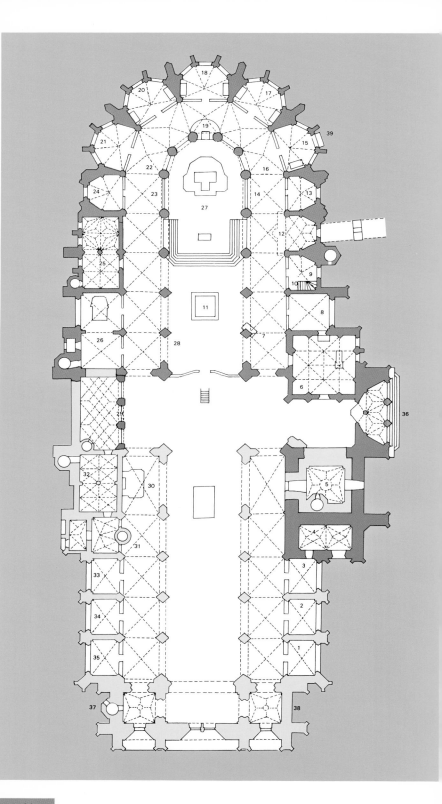

Red building – Matthias of Arras

Blue building – Peter Parler

Green masonry – Renaissance

Yellow masonry – 19th century

The main nave. A big pointed window with a rosette stands out in the western wall of the main nave. Its glazing symbolizes the creation of the world after a design by F. Kysela. Remaining in the centre of the Neo-Gothic nave is an elevated

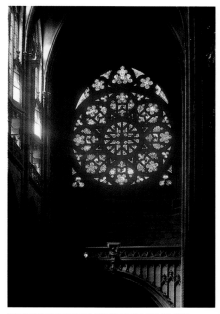

ROSETTE IN THE WESTERN FAÇADE
(dia. 10.6 m)

console for the uncompleted tombstone of St. Adalbert, whose bodily remains were interred in the planned main nave. (The competition organized in 1938 for the design of a new tombstone for St. Adalbert was won by K. Vobišová, but her idea was never realized.)

The transverse nave. This nave is of the same height as the main nave and forms the boundary between the old and the new part of the cathedral. On the pillars of the intersecting point of the main and transverse naves there are eight gilded wooden statues of Czech provincial saints, which originally stood on the pillars of the choir. These saints are Vitus, John Nepomuk, Sigimund, Adalbert, Ludmila, Wenceslas, Procopius and Norbert. They are the work of T. Becker of 1606 after designs by F. Preiss.

POINT OF INTERSECTION OF THE MAIN AND THE TRANSVERSE NAVE

The northern branch of the transverse nave. Since 1924 the music choir has been situated here. It is the work of B. Wolmut of 1557–1561. Originally it closed the western side of the completed part of the chancel on the western side. Situated on its ground-floor is the Choir Chapel. Two of its three big oak doors, specifically the side ones, date in 1639, while the middle one was added in 1929 after a design by Š. Záležák. The chapel has an interesting net vault with ribs partially loosely suspended below it. Of the interior furnishings it is particularly the high altar that attracts attention. It is composed of two parts built over an interval of 350 years. The architecture of the altar dates in 1579 and originally it formed the frame of M. Pychler's painted epitaph. In the period during which the painting was missing the sculptor J. Horejc filled the empty frame with a relief The Crucifixion and a sculpture Christ's Resurrection. Two years later, however, the painting was found, but it was returned to the cathedral in a new frame and in a different place. The archbishop's throne of the first half of the 17th century originally stood by the high altar as the counterpart of the imperial throne, which is now in the

collections of the Prague Museum. The arcade on the first floor of the music choir has a rib vault. The big organ in the choir is the work of A. Gärtner of Tachov of 1763 and it has Rococo decoration. Now, however, it is incomplete and cannot be played.

The southern branch of the transverse nave. Situated here are marble tombstones and the relief memorial to the fallen, the work of K. Pokorný of 1921. Standing nearby is a holy-water sprinkler of red marble and a green-marbled serpentine with a bronze statue of the young St. Wenceslas, the work of K. Dvořák of 1929. The southern wall is broken up by a glazed grille-type entrance, produced after a design by J. Sokol of 1955. Hanging above it is the gilded relief emblem of the capital Prague, the work of K. Štipl of 1946. On the left of the entrance there is a painting The Removal from the Cross of the 17th century. Near the corner of St. Wenceslas's Chapel stands a statue of Jesus Christ of Karar marble (Č. Vosmík, 1897). The whole of the upper part of the southern front of the transverse nave is filled with an enormous window with Neo-Gothic tracery and the St. Wenceslas crown executed in stone at its top. The glazing, produced after designs by

M. Švabinský in 1939, portrays The Last Judgement. Certain Czech rulers are portrayed in the group of the chosen: Charles IV and his consort, Václav IV, George of Poděbrady, Ladislav Pohrobek, Rudolph II and Ferdinand I.

The choir. Standing separately in front of the high altar in the choir of the cathedral is the royal mausoleum, a large tomb of white marble. It was hewn by the Netherlandish sculptor A. Colin in Innsbruck. The work was completed in 1589. The finished parts were transported by boat and sledge to Prague, where they were assembled. Reclining on the upper surface of the tomb are the figures of Ferdinand I (in the centre), his consort Anne Jagiello and his son Maxmilián II. The sculptor portrayed all three figures in great detail down to the plastic patterns of the materials and the decoration of the armour. On the western side of the mausoleum stands a statue of Christ the Saviour, its periphery being lined with putti with escutcheons. The side walls of the tomb are decorated with eight medallions with reliefs of the rulers who were interred in royal tombs below the mausoleum in the late 16th century: Charles IV, his four consorts, Václav IV, Ladislav Pohrobek and George of Poděbrady.

STATUES OF ST. LUDMILA AND ST. WENCESLAS

The forged Renaissance grille surrounding the mausoleum was formed from rods twisted into scrolls and braids by a Little Quarter locksmith by the name of J. Schmidthammer.

TRANSVERSE NAVE

VAULT OF THE CHOIR CHAPEL

ALTAR IN THE CHOIR CHAPEL

HIGH ALTAR

The furnishings of the choir. Built-on to a pillar near the mausoleum is a <u>pulpit</u> of 1631, richly decorated with engraving, painting and gilding. The <u>Baroque pews</u> in the choir also have rich engraved decorations. The <u>high altar</u> on a foot with steps originated after a design by J. Kranner, but was changed by J. Mocker. Its Neo-Gothic architecture was hewn from cretaceous marly limestone. The delicate Neo-Gothic reliquaries and candlesticks were decorated with enamels by J. Chadt.

The windows of the choir. The three windows in the east end of the choir are filled with a <u>large composition The Holiest Trinity (in the centre) with saints and donors. M. Švabinský's designs, created in the course of World War II, were</u> realized from 1946 to 1948. The glazing of the window on the left-hand side portrays the figures of the Blessed Mlada Přemyslovna, Our Lady with the St. Wenceslas crown and St. Ludmila. Below them can be seen the figure of Prince Spytihněv II with a model of St. Vitus's Basilica. In the glazing of the right-hand window can be seen the patron saints St. Wenceslas and St. Vitus and, as a donor, Charles IV with a model of the Gothic cathedral.

DOOR OF THE CHOIR CHAPEL

SOUTHERN BRANCH
OF THE TRANSVERSE NAVE

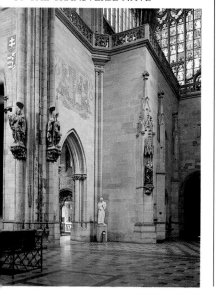

DETAIL OF THE ROYAL MAUSOLEUM

CONSOLE WITH LUNA
ON THE HIGH ALTAR

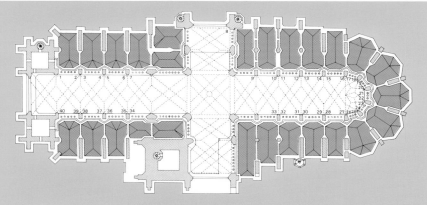

INNER TRIFORIUM

1. Kamil Hilbert
2. Josef Kranner
3. Jan Javůrek, president of the Union
4. František Thun-Hohenstein
5. Archbishop František Kordač
6. Archbishop František Schönborn
7. František Thun-Hohenstein
8. Maskaron
9. Maskaron
10. Maskaron
11. Václav of Radeč
12. Matthias of Arras
13. Peter Parler
14. Ondřej Kotlík
15. Beneš Krabice of Weitmile
16. Václav Luxembourg
17. Jan Jindřich, margrave of Moravia, brother of Charles IV
18. Blanche of Valois
19. Anne of the Palatinate
20. Anna Svídnická
21. Elizabeth of Pomorania
22. Charles IV
23. John of Luxembourg
24. Eliška Přemyslovna
25. Václav IV, son of Charles IV
26. Johanna of Bavaria
27. Arnošt of Pardubice
28. Jan Očko of Vlašim
29. Jan of Jenštejn
30. Mikuláš Holubec
31. Bušek Leonardův
32. A griffin
33. A cat and a dog
34. Václav Michal Pešina of Čechorod, founder of the Union
35. Archbishop Bedřich Josef Schwarzenberg
36. Sanctifying Bishop Antonín Podlaha
37. Bedřich Thun-Hohenstein, president of the Union
38. Vojtěch Schönborn
39. Josef Mocker
40. Josef Zlatník

BUST OF MATTHIAS OF ARRAS
ON THE TRIFORIUM

◄ THE WINDOW'S OF THE HIGH CHOIR

The inner triforium. This triforium runs above the arches of the arcades between the main and the side aisles. In the Gothic part of the cathedral people originally passed through passageways in the supporting pillars, but these were walled-up in the 19th century for static reasons. Hewn above these passagways were portrait busts of members of the imperial family and persons deserving merit for the construction of the cathedral. Here artists employed at Peter Parler's St. Vitus workshop created exceptionally effective and momentous sculptures which had no like in Europe at their time. On the same level, regardless of their rank at birth, they portray, apart from the Emperor Charles IV and all his

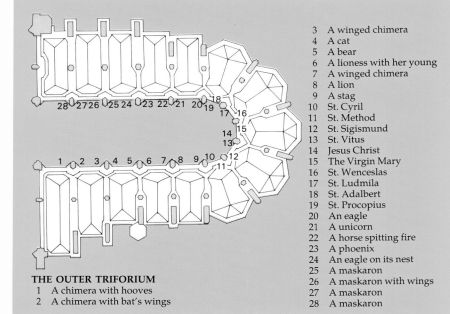

3 A winged chimera
4 A cat
5 A bear
6 A lioness with her young
7 A winged chimera
8 A lion
9 A stag
10 St. Cyril
11 St. Method
12 St. Sigismund
13 St. Vitus
14 Jesus Christ
15 The Virgin Mary
16 St. Wenceslas
17 St. Ludmila
18 St. Adalbert
19 St. Procopius
20 An eagle
21 A unicorn
22 A horse spitting fire
23 A phoenix
24 An eagle on its nest
25 A maskaron
26 A maskaron with wings
27 A maskaron
28 A maskaron

THE OUTER TRIFORIUM
1 A chimera with hooves
2 A chimera with bat's wings

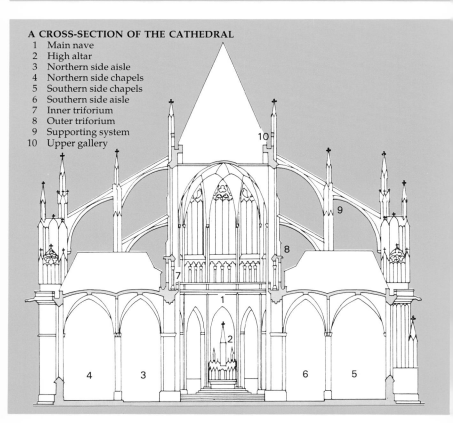

A CROSS-SECTION OF THE CATHEDRAL
1 Main nave
2 High altar
3 Northern side aisle
4 Northern side chapels
5 Southern side chapels
6 Southern side aisle
7 Inner triforium
8 Outer triforium
9 Supporting system
10 Upper gallery

SCULPTURED PORTRAIT OF CHARLES IV ON THE TRIFORIUM ▶

consorts, Charles's parents, his son Václav IV with his consort, Duke Václav Luxembourg and Jan Jindřich, margrave of Moravia, three archbishops and both architects and all five supervisors of the building work. This gallery of portrait busts is supplemented with two animal motifs and three sculptured masks. The triforium of the new part of the cathedral is also decorated with busts. They were to have been arranged analogically, as in the medieval triforium, but the year 1918 definitely excluded the possibility of providing space for the busts of the imperial family. For this reason portraits of persons deserving the greatest credit for the completion of the cathedral were sculptured. Apart from all three architects, Kranner, Mocker and Hilbert, their number includes archbishops and important functionaries of the Union for the Completion of the Cathedral. The works were entrusted to the younger generation of Czech sculptors (B. Kafka, J. Štursa, J. Lauda, B. Benda, J. Kavan, J. Kofránek).

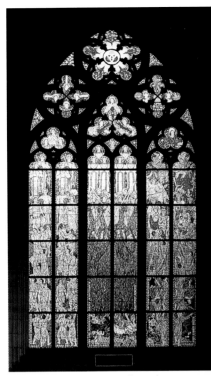

WINDOW OF ST. ANNA ČESKÁ'S CHAPEL

WINDOW OF ST. LUDMILA'S CHAPEL

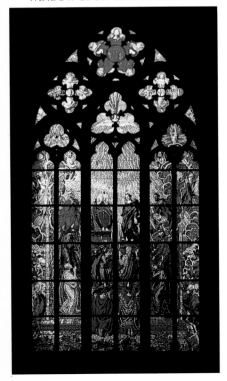

The outer triforium. The gallery of the outer triforium runs above the inner triforium on its outer side. Here, too, the original passageways in the pillars were walled-up in the 19th century. Above them are consoles with reliefs of fantastic animals and faces. The eastern side is reserved for busts of Christ, the Virgin Mary and the chief provincial saints (SS. Vitus, Wenceslas, Adalbert, Procopius, Ludmila, Cyril and Method, Sigismund).

The arcade walls of the choir. On the arcade walls of the choir, below the tracery balustrade of the inner triforium, are the painted provincial emblems. They symbolize the titles of the rulers of the Hapsburg dynasty in the 16th and 17th centuries. Adjoining them are memorial inscriptions, written in Latin, about the history of the construction of the cathedral and, from the time of its completion, Czech inscriptions with the emblems of the countries of the First Republic.

The side chapels
in the southern nave

Panels with the plastic ground-plans of the excavations of St. Vitus's Rotunda and Basilica are to be seen behind the main entrance below the south-west steeple. The glazing of the window portrays the figures of SS. Elizabeth, Barbara and Adolph, realized after a design by C. Bouda in 1931.

St. Ludmila's Chapel (Baptismal)
A continuous row of side chapels begins on the southern side. It is closed with a gilded bronze grille made by J. Horejc in 1938. The decoration of its walls and window was designed by M. Švabinský. His window with the theme The Sending-down of the Holy Spirit of 1934 to 1935 is colourfully effective. The western wall is decorated with a mosaic The Baptism of Christ, realized in 1953. (The design of a mosaic The Transfiguration of the Lord on Mount Tabor, intended for placing on the opposite wall, has not been realized to date.) The cretaceous

WINDOW OF THE CHAPEL
OF GOD'S SEPULCHRE

marly limestone altar was executed after a design by J. Kranner, the statue of St. Ludmila having been hewn from Karar marble by E. Max in 1845. The altar has stood here since 1921, having previously been situated in the axial chapel of the choir gallery. The Baroque serpentine font comes from the furnishings of St. Wenceslas's Chapel. The bronze sculpture portraying The Baptism of St. Ludmila above it is the work of K. Pokorný of 1935. The painting The Burial of Christ is attributed to an unknown Italian painter of the 17th century.

The Chapel of God's Sepulchre
The coloured window with the theme The Performance of Deeds of Charity originated after a design by K. Svolinský in 1932. The Early Baroque altar of 1674 was transferred here from St. Anne's Chapel in St. George's Convent. The painting St. Mary Magdalene was painted about 1600 by A. Lomi and the painting The Holy Family with Angels on the southern wall is the work of an unknown painter of the latter half of the 17th century.

Thun Chapel. The figural coloured window with the theme of the psalm "He Who Sows in Tears Shall Reap in Joy" was designed by F. Kysela in 1928 to 1929. The Neo-Classical altar is decorated with an older painting The Dead Christ with Angels by one of the masters of the Rudolphian circle. The wooden reliefs (St. Margaret and St. Ursula) hanging on the wall date in the early 16th century, the three others having been carved by L. Boček in 1942. The door in the corner leads to the chapter library; the collection of valuable manscripts and prints is currently housed in the more suitable and safer interiors of Prague Castle.

Hazmburg Chapel. This chapel forms the ground-floor of the great steeple and therefore does not open fully into the interior. In the solid wall there are several Renaissance tombstones of cretaceous marly limestone and Slivenec marble. Chapel with St. František Serafinský, Charles Borromaeus and the principal. The coloured window of 1934, designed by C. Bouda, portrays the laying of the foundation stone of the completion of the building (1873) and is provided with a panel with explanations.

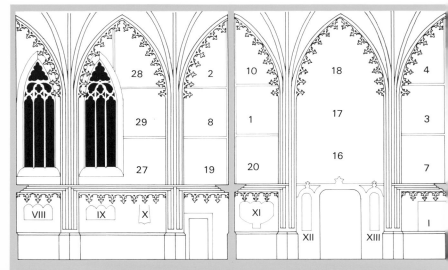

WALL PAINTINGS IN ST. WENCESLAS'S CHAPEL

I	Christ on the Mount of Olives	VII	Christ on the cross
II	Christ's captivity	VIII	Christ in the sepulchre
III	Christ in front of Pilate	IX	The Resurrection
IV	The flagellation of Christ	X	The Assumption
V	Christ crowned with a crown of thorns	XI	The sending-down of the Holy Spirit
VI	The crucifixion with the Virgin Mary, St. John and donors	XII	St. Paul
		XIII	St. Peter

1 St. Wenceslas redeeming pagan children
2 having them christened
3 cutting-down the gallows
4 visiting prisoners
5 letting them out of prison
6 satiating travellers
7 burying the dead
8 officiating during a mass
9 bringing wood to a widow and being maltreated by gamekeepers
10 advising Podiven to follow in his footsteps in the snow
11 ploughing a field
12 sowing corn

The great steeple

The Hazmburg Chapel serves mainly as the <u>entrance to the observation gallery</u> of the great steeple, from where a spiral staircase with 287 steps runs.

The bells. On the first floor of the steeple there hangs the <u>biggest of the St. Vitus bells, Zikmund,</u> the work of T. Jaroš decorated with figural reliefs of 1549. It is the third bell to bear this name and to boast this size: the first was destroyed during its transport to the Castle in 1534 and the second during the fire of 1541. Hanging on the second floor are three small Renaissance bells: Václav, John the Baptist and Joseph.

The clock. A clockwork of the late 16th century, repaired in 1930, is situated on the highest floor of the steeple.

St. Wenceslas's Chapel

St. Wenceslas's Chapel partially projects into the transverse nave. Its exceptional importance is reflected in the wholly different conception of its architecture and magnificent decoration. Everything was intended to emphasize the fact that just <u>this chapel is the central point of the</u>

13 harvesting and threshing corn
14 baking hosts
15 pressing grapes
16 arriving at the Diet
17 St. Wenceslas, accompanied by angels, being welcomed by the Emperor Jindřich Ptáčník
18 The imperial electors awaiting the arrival of the emperor and St. Wenceslas
19 St. Wenceslas receiving the relics of St. Vitus
20 placing them ceremoniously in the altar of the rotunda
21 arranging a duel with Radslav, prince of Zlik
22 Radslav humbles himself in front of St. Wenceslas
23 The welcoming of St. Wenceslas at Stará Boleslav
24 The banquet at Stará Boleslav
25 The murder of St. Wenceslas
26 The miracle during the transport of St. Wenceslas's body
27 Podiven kills St. Wenceslas's murderer at the baths and is hung
28 Christ appears to King Erik of Denmark and orders him to build St. Wenceslas's Church
29 King Erik inspects the completed church
30 Portrait of King Vladislav Jagiello
31 Portrait of Queen Anne de Foix-Candale
32 Statue of St. Wenceslas
33 St. Sigismund and St. Vitus
34 St. Adalbert and St. Ludmila

cathedral as a whole with the tomb of the most important provincial patron saint.

The shape of the chapel. The chapel has a square ground-plan and a net vault whose ribs pass uninterruptedly into supports situated beyond the corners of the chapel. The lower part of the walls below the huge, profiled cornice bears original Gothic decoration of the late Sixties of the 14th century.

The decoration of the walls. Their panelling of precious stones of a then contemporary conception symbolized Heavenly Jerusalem. Wall paintings of the Passion cycle are

STATUE OF ST. WENCESLAS

composed in it. The creators of the panelling cut the small panels of red jasper, purple amethyst and green chrysoprase with the aid of a thin cable and grinding powder and after polishing them arranged them so as to form the constantly repeated motif of a cross. The gaps between them are decorated with plastic gilded designs. Above the altar painting, whose front wall is still of Gothic origin, there is a wall painting The Crucifixion with the figures of the donors, Charles IV and Elizabeth of Pomerania.

The surfaces of the walls above the cornice are covered with Scenes from the Life of St. Wenceslas. The individual scenes, of which there thirty-one, are not grouped chronologically. They are attributed to the workshop of the Master of the Litoměřice Altar and date in 1509. In

FLAMING FEMALE EAGLE ON THE WESTERN DOOR OF THE CHAPEL

CZECH CORONATION JEWELS

◄ WALL PAINTINGS IN ST. WENCESLAS'S CHAPEL

BRONZE CANDLESTICK

1614 they were discovered by Daniel Alexius of Květná, who supplemented them with the coats-of-arms and names of the persons who financed their repair. (The St. Wenceslas legend does not contain only portraits of King Vladislav Jagiello and his consort Anne de Foix-Candale by the sides of the window in the eastern wall.)

St. Wenceslas's tomb. St. Wenceslas's tomb, combined with an altar, is situated in the chapel. It is a modern reconstruction designed by Kamil Hilbert in the years 1912 to 1913 after the partially preserved tomb of the time of Charles IV.

The cretaceous marly limestone statue of St. Wenceslas situated on the cornice above the altar is most likely the work of Henry Parler of 1373. Some of its details were supplemented during its modern restoration: the polychrome is wholly new.

The St. Vitus pastoforium. Standing in the south-eastern corner on a Neo-Gothic pedestal is the St. Vitus pastoforium, a tower-shaped container for the safe-keeping of the altar sacraments. It is the work of Parler's workshop and, similarly as the grille of the recess next to the altar, is made of gilded green plate.

Other furnishings of the chapel. The gilded chandelier and forged door of the western entrance date in the early 20th century. The northern portal of the chapel, including the door, is of Gothic origin: the knocker in the form

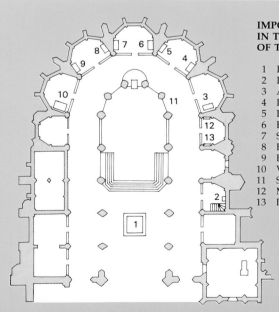

**IMPORTANT TOMBS
IN THE CHOIR
OF THE CATHEDRAL**

1 Royal mausoleum
2 Rudolph I called Gruel
3 Archbishop Jan Očko of Vlašim
4 Přemysl Otakar I
5 Přemysl Otakar II
6 Břetislav I
7 Spytihněv II
8 Břetislav II
9 Bořivoj II
10 Vratislav of Pernštejn
11 St. John Nepomuk
12 Matthias of Arras
13 Peter Parler

ROYAL ORATORY

of a lion's head was allegedly brought here from Stará Boleslav. Standing next to the northern entrance is a large bronze candlestick with a statue of St. Wenceslas, the work of Hans Vischer of Nuremberg of 1532. Hanging on the neighbouring pillar is a panel painting The Murder of St. Wenceslas of 1543 by the owner of the monogram IW.

The door to the crown chamber. The door in the south-western corner of the chapel dates in 1867 and is provided with seven locks. It leads to the crown chamber, in which the Czech coronation jewels are kept.

The choir chapels
The Martinic Chapel (St. Andrew's). This chapel was built on a right-angled ground-plan as one of the open choir chapels. Just as all the other choir chapels, it has a gilded forged grille dating from before the mid-18th century. The large window with the figures of saints dates in 1880. It was designed by J. Mocker and F. Sequens. The wall paintings with scenes from the life of St. Andrew are also the work of F. Sequens. The marble Neo-Gothic altar was built in 1873 by T. V. Achtermann. On the western wall, high above the floor, is the epitaph of Jan Popel of Lobkowicz, the supreme steward of the kingdom. It was

sculptured by V. Strašryba of Louny from 1581 to 1582, use being made of white and red marble. In the wall there are the epitaphs of the lords of Martinic of 1624. Among them is also the tablet of Jaroslav Bořita, one of the defenestrated governors. The tombstone of the supreme chancellor Leopold Count Šlik on a pillar opposite the chapel originated in 1723 with

HANGING COPING STONE
OF THE ORATORY

the cooperation of J. E. Fischer of Erlach, F. Kaňka and M. B. Braun. On the console of the next pillar there is a wooden polychromed statue of Our Lady Dolorous of Renaissance origin.

The Chapel of the Holy Rood (SS. Simon and Juda). Matthias of Arras began to build this chapel as a polygonal type and Peter Parler completed it as a right-angled one. The coloured window of 1869 is the work of A. Lhota and J. Z. Quast. The partially preserved Gothic painting on the wall portrays the enthroned Madonna with Child, surrounded by angels, saints and kneeling donors. Hanging above it is the so-called

CZECH EMBLEM ON THE PORTAL BELOW THE ORATORY

Milanese Cross, a carving of Italian origin. A marble panel in the floor reminds the viewer of the grave of King Rudolph I. Royal burial insignia of gilded silver were found in the grave, discovered in 1870.

The Royal Oratory. This oratory originated in one of the choir chapels after 1490. It is most likely the work of H. Spiess and B. Ried. The interesting vault with a protruding coping stone has naturalistically executed dry, cut branches, tied with strong ropes at the top of the arches, instead of ribs. The balustrade of the oratory with suspended provincial emblems is also of illusive branches. In 1878 a copy of its eastern half, damaged during the insertion of the younger, glazed oratory, was made of wood.

On the pillar of the Royal Oratory and on that of the opposite pillar stand two polychromed statues of Kutná Hora miners from M. B. Braun's workshop (1721–1725).

Wallenstein Chapel (St. Mary Magdalena's. The Most Sacred Heart of Our Lord and Our Lady). The preserved part of the Gothic wall paintings portrays the Virgin Mary with the Child Jesus, saints and kneeling donors. The remaining paintings are from as late as 1905 to 1907 and are the work of Z. Rudl. The figural coloured window of 1880, made after a design by F. Sequens, depicts St. Mary Magdalene washing Christ's feet; the erect figures are St. Bartholomew and St. Matthew. For the building of the altar use was made of a part of the Early Baroque altar of the archbishop Sobek of Bilenberk from St. Wenceslas's Chapel (built in 1673 and transferred in 1911). In the 17th century St.

LEOPOLD ŠLIK'S EPITAPH

TOMB OF JAN OČKO OF VLAŠIM

WALL PAINTING IN THE SAXON CHAPEL

Wenceslas's helmet was kept in its upper wooden and gilded extension. The <u>raised tombstones of the builders of the cathedral Matthias of Arras and Peter Parler</u> were transferred here from their original site in the paving in front of the old sacristy.

Set between pillars on the <u>gallery opposite the chapel</u> is a <u>two-part relief</u> portraying the devastation of St. Vitus's Cathedral by the Calvinists during the reign of Fridrich of the Palatinate in 1619. The carving is the work of J. Bendl of the Thirties of the 17th century.

The Chapel of St. John Nepomuk (the Vlašim Chapel). This chapel has a relatively simple, modern <u>altar,</u> which is decorated with silver busts of four Czech patron saints – Wenceslas, Adalbert, Cyril and Vitus. It was presented to the chapel by the then archbishop Jan Josef Breunel in 1699. Built-on on to a side wall is the <u>tomb</u> of Prague's second bishop, <u>Jan Očko of Vlašim.</u> The tombstone is of red marble with the reclining figure of the archbishop with a dog at his foot of white marble. The poly-chromed relief <u>emblems in the wall</u> above the tombstone also belong to Jan Očko, who was the bishop of Olomouc (the emblem with a mitre), the archbishop of Prague (the middle

TOMB OF ST. JOHN NEPOMUK

emblem) and the cardinal (the family coat-of-arms with a cardinal's hat by the pillar of the vault). Partly preserved on the walls of the chapel are <u>wall paintings</u> of the 14th century: on the western wall Dolorous Christ, a scene The Beheading of St. Catherine. St. Adalbert and on the eastern wall a scene The Baptism of St. Otilie. The kneeling figure of Jan Očko can be seen in the lower part of both scenes, once as the archbishop and in the second case in the garments of the cardinal. The coloured <u>windows</u> with mainly ornamental decoration were designed in 1871 by J. Kranner, R. Müller and P. Meisner. The glazing of the windows has ornamental motifs with small figures of saints. The middle window shows St. John Nepomuk and three scenes from his life.

On the <u>gallery opposite the chapel</u> can be seen the big <u>silver tomb of St. John Nepomuk.</u> It was made from 1733 to 1736 by the silversmith J. J. Würth of Vienna after a design by the architect J. E. Fischer of Erlach and

TOMB OF PŘEMYSL OTAKAR I

TOMB OF PŘEMYSL OTAKAR II

the modeller A. Corradini. Set in place on the sides of the pedestal are four reliefs from the life of the saint and reliefs of the virtues. At the top two kneeling angels are raising a coffin with the kneeling figure of St. John Nepomuk on the lid. The balustrade of variously coloured marble with vases and allegorical figures on separate pillars was built round the tomb additionally (1746). The baldachin and the suspended figures of four flying angels were added in 1771. The simple forged balustrade dates in 1983.

The Saxon Chapel (The Chapel of the Holy Relics, Šternberk Chapel). The western wall of the chapel is decorated with a wall painting The Adoration of the Three Kings, preserved from the time of Charles IV. Set in the opposite wall is a relief portrayal of the Saxon emblem, hewn from sandstone and polychromed. The glazing of the windows was designed jointly by J. Mocker and F. Sequens in 1878. It is divided up by rich architecture with the figures of the Virgin Mary and the Child Jesus, angels and another eleven saints. The chapel altar is composed of various parts. The relief-decorated table is Gothic and resting on it is a Baroque cabinet with numerous components for relics. Standing by the side walls are the cretaceous marly limestone tombs of Czech kings, created by artists of Peter Parler's workshop in the Seventies of the 14th century. The figure of Přemysl Otakar I on the tomb on the left is the work of Peter Parler. Its counterpart is a tomb with the figure of "the iron and gold king"

Přemysl Otakar II. His military attire brings to mind the fact that he fell in the Battle of Moravské pole. Royal burial insignia of gilded silver were placed in Přemysl Otakar II's grave.

The Chapel of Our Lady (The Chapel of the Holiest Trinity, of the Berks of Dubá, of the Rood and of St. Ludmila). This chapel is situated in the centre, in the axis of the choir and the building as a whole. Above the grille, which closes the chapel, there is a beam with a group of statues The Calvary by the wood-carver D. Altmann of Eydenburk of 1621. The group of statues was presented to the cathedral by Ferdinand II after his victory in the Battle of the White Mountain. The wall paintings are the work of F. Sequens and A. Krisan of 1895 to 1898 and they portray scenes from the life of the Virgin Mary and a scene showing the transfer of the relics of St. Vitus and their presentation to the cathedral (the lower, uncoloured field). The coloured windows with figures of saints and The Holiest Trinity were designed by J. Mocker and F. Sequens. The altar, likewise built after a design by J. Mocker, has the form of a Gothic ark with reliefs by J. Kastner and painted decoration by A. Krisan. The most momentous monuments in the chapel are, however, the tomb-stones of Prince Břetislav I in knight's armour (the bodily remains of his consort Jitka were laid to rest in a casket below the tomb) and Prince Spytihněv II in a long cloak. Both tombstones were produced from cretaceous marly limestone at Parler's workshop.

In 1840 the <u>tombstone of St. Vitus, combined with an altar,</u> was built <u>on the gallery in front of the chapel</u> (also in the axis of the cathedral). A sandstone statue of the saint, the work of E. Max executed in sandstone after a design by J. Kranner, stands on the architecture. Set in the paving in front of the tomb are <u>fourteen gravestones of Prague's bishops.</u> Their remains were brought here in 1374 by Beneš Krabice of Weitmile from the old basilica consecrated to St. Vitus.

The Chapel of St. John the Baptist (the Chapel of Arnošt of Pardubice and of St. Anthony the Hermit). Of all the choir chapels this is the only one not to have been preserved in its original Gothic form. Its foundations were so shallow and its walls so

STATUE OF CARDINAL
BEDŘICH SCHWARZENBERG

destroyed that it was necessary to newly build it (1863–1864). This explains why the masonry of this chapel differs conspicuously from that of the medieval parts. The <u>marble tombs of two of Prague's bishops</u> were walled-in in the walls without murals. (Antonín Brus of Mohelnice (†1580) and Martin Medek (†1590) were the first to be installed in the office of Prague's archbishop, which had been unoccupied since the Hussite wars.) The walls are further decorated with <u>paintings</u> – St. Philip

of Neri by J. J. Q. Jahn (1772) and The Death St. Joseph by F. Trevisan (1656) and below it a Baroque wooden relief The Crucifixion in a glazed frame. The coloured <u>glazing of the windows</u> was designed by J. Z. Quast in cooperation with A. Lhota and J. M. Trenkwald. Standing by the side walls are the <u>tombs of Czech princes from the Přemyslid dynasty,</u> which originated in the Seventies of the 14th century. Contrary to the others, the figures on the upper tablets are hewn on a somewhat smaller scale. Břetislav II (†1100) is portrayed in knight's armour and Bořivoj II (†1124) in a cloak. The chapel <u>altar</u> dates in 1876. It was built of sandstone after designs by J. Kranner and J. Mocker. The statues of St. John the Baptist and St. Cyril were sculptured by V. Levý, while the sculpture of St. Method is the work of J. V. Myslbek. <u>Between pillars on the gallery</u> opposite the chapel hangs a <u>painting of St. John Nepomuk</u> of the late 17th century. In the foreground the saint is being judged by King Václav IV, the queen's confession is portrayed on the left and in the background St. John is being thrown into the River Vltava.

OLD SACRISTY

The Pernštejn Chapel (the Old Archbishop's Chapel). The wall paintings on the theme of the life of St. Adalbert were painted after designs by F. Sequens in 1888 to 1890. The coloured figural glazings of the windows originated in the cooperation of the painter F. Sequens and the architect J. Mocker ten years earlier. Adjoining the western wall of the chapel is the big tomb of Vratislav of Pernštejn, the supreme chancellor of the kingdom (1582). The tomb is hewn of red marble and there is a relief figure of the deceased on the upper slab. Other tombs document the fact that the Prague archbishops were buried in this chapel in the years 1793 to 1899. The Neo-Gothic altar was designed by J. Mocker and it was built in 1898 with the participation of V. Mráz (the architecture of the altar), J. Kastner (the statues and reliefs) and Z. Rudl (the painted decoration).

On the gallery of the choir opposite the chapel there is a bronze statue of Cardinal Bedřich Josef Schwarzenberg, archbishop of Prague. It is the work of J. V. Myslbek of 1891 to 1895. The two big oak panels with reliefs by J. Bendl hung on the wall between the pillars of the choir represent The Flight of Fridrich of the Palatinate After the Battle of the White Mountain. A unique portrayal of Prague Castle from the north forms a part of the relief.

St. Anne's Chapel (the Nostic Chapel). The cycle of wall paintings with the theme of the life of St. Anne and the design of the figural decoration of the window (the family tree of the Virgin Mary) are the work of J. Swerts of 1878 to 1880. On the coping stone of the rib vault there is the relief emblem of the lords of Dražice (Jan IV of Dražice was the last bishop of Prague) and on that of the vault of the gallery in front of the chapel the emblem of the lords of Pardubice (Arnošt of Pardubice was Prague's first archbishop). The altar, designed by J. Mocker, was built in Neo-Gothic style from 1878 to 1980. A relics panel of 1266 forms a part of the altar. This valuable monument became a part of the St. Vitus treasure in 1988. A precise copy of it has been made for the altar.

ST. SIGISMUND'S ALTAR

TOMBSTONES
IN ST. SIGISMUND'S CHAPEL

BÍLEK'S ALTAR

STAIRCASE LEADING
TO HILBERT'S TREASURY

The Old Sacristy (St. Michael's Chapel.) This part has its original Gothic entrance with blind tracery above it. Standing next to the entrance on a console is a wooden, polychromed statue of the Archangle Michael. It. originated in South Ger-

many in the early 17th century. Above the Baroque confessional the following paintings are to be seen hanging on the wall: Christ's Entry Into Jerusalem (copy of the 17th century after Tizian), St. Maurice by J. K. Liška (of the late 17th century), on the left of the entrance to the sacristy The Baptism of Christ by P. Brandl (1722) and The Visitation of the Virgin Mary by J. J. Hering (c. 1630). – The sacristy has an oblong ground-plan divided into two halves by a pillar. Each half has a different rib vault with a hanging coping stone. These two vaults, characterized by a very complicated design, were built by Parler's workshop. The shape of the vault in the eastern field was determined by a now unknown predecessor of Parler who began the construction of the sacristy. The western field was closed by a simpler vault which was wholly realized after a design by Peter Parler. A spiral staircase in the north-west corner of the sacristy leads to the treasury where the St. Vitus treasure was originally kept.

St. Sigismund's Chapel (Černín Chapel). This chapel is the last of the choir chapels built in the Middle Ages. However, its appearance is quite different. It is approximately as big as the neighbouring Old Sacristy, but its vault is higher and open into the cathedral. The wall painting of the Assumption of Our Lady on the western wall is dated in the late 16th century. The opposite wall is decorated with a cycle of paintings with scenes from the life of St. Sigismund of the same period. It is attributed to Daniel Alexius of Květná, who also worked in St. Wenceslas's Chapel. A considerable part of the paintings on the eastern wall is covered by a big Baroque altar. It originated in the Thirties of the 18th century after a design by the architect F. M. Kaňka and was decorated with carved adornments by F. I. Weiss. The window in the eastern half of the chapel with the figures of St. Sigismund and another five saints was designed by A. Lhota (1870), while the window in the western half

WINDOW
OF THE NEW ARCHBISHOP'S PALACE ▶

was jointly designed in 1875 by J. Mocker (architecture) and F. Sequens (the figures of three saints). Most important among the tombs set in the walls of the chapel are those of Humprecht Jan Černín of Chudenice of 1682 (architecture with spiral columns on the western wall), Prince Sigismund Bathory of Transylvania of 1613 (in the northern wall) and the epitaph of don Antonio de Cardono and his wife of 1553 (in the eastern wall behind the altar).

**The side chapels
in the northern aisle**

The northern band of side chapels in the Neo-Gothic part of the cathedral continues beyond the transverse nave (with Wolmut's choir) in north-westerly direction.

The New Sacristy. The closed interior of the New Sacristy takes up the width of two chapels beyond the transverse nave. It has cross vaults borne by two huge granite columns. Placed below the vault are eight copies of busts of Czech patron saints from the outer triforium. They are the work of V. Levý and were intended to replace the originals, but this change was never realized. By the wall which closes off the New Sacristy from the interior of the cathedral there is an altar created by F. Bílek. While the relief The Crucifixion dates in 1899, the other parts of the altar were made by F. Bílek in 1927. Hanging on the sides of the altar are bronze relief epitaphs: on the left of Jan Dlasek of Vchynice (†1521) and on the right of Helferich Gutsulber (†1585).

The neighbouring norther vestibule is not used as an entrance. A broken spiral staircase with K. Hilbert's monogram and the date 1927 above the portal passes between the two entrances. It leads to a landing affording access to the New (Hilbert's) Treasury, where, behind safe-type doors, the greater part of the articles forming the St. Vitus treasure are kept in special glass cabinets. The installation was completed in 1929 and for a certain time the treasure was also accessible to the public. Above the landing, in front of the treasury, there is a coloured window by C. Bouda with scenes from the life of St. Stephen.

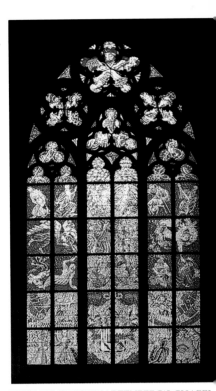

WINDOW OF SCHWARZENBERG'S CHAPEL

The New Archbishop's Hora's Chapel. The chapel window, designed by A. Mucha in 1931, portrays scenes from the life of SS. Cyril and Method and due to its colours it differs conspicuously from the other windows. The altar table of 1673 was transferred here in 1929 and supplemented with an extension with a transfer of the wall painting The Assumption of Our Lady by B. Spranger (1593). The crypt below the chapel serves as the grave of the Prague archbishops and has been used as such since 1909. Buried here to date have been Archbishop F. Kordač (†1931), Cardinal K. Kašpar (†1941) and Cardinal F. Tomášek (†1991) and with them the sanctifying Bishop A. Podlaha (†1932).

Schwarzenberg Chapel. The coloured glazing of the window is the work of K. Svolinský of 1930 to 1931. Its central motif is The Holiest Trinity and the coat-of-arms of the Schwarzenberg family. The altar was built in 1938, but its main part is the so-called Čimelice ark with The Adoration of the Three Kings of the early 16th century. The opposite wall is decorated with a panel painting The Resurrection of Christ with the kneeling figure of the Silesian nobleman Mikuláš Pychler, to whose epitaph it belonged. The painting is attributed to B. Spranger and dated in the last quarter of the 16th century. The youngest feature in the chapel is the bronze panel with the coat-of-arms of the Schwarzenberg family, set in place here to commemorate the events of November and December 1989 which led to the fall of the communist regime in Czechoslovakia.

St. Agnes's Chapel (the Chapel of the Bartoň family of Dobenín). This chapel is the last in the row of northern side chapels. It was consecrated by the Prague archbishop František Cardinal Tomášek in 1989 to the just sanctified Czech saint. The mosaics on the walls are the work of F. Kysela and date in the years 1934 to 1935. They portray allegories of beatitude. This theme was also used in the glazing of the window, again designed by F. Kysela. The chapel is closed by K. Štipl's grille of 1937. The altar was built of North Italian Gothic arks and a modern table of Slivenec marble. The wall painting of the Bartoň family on the northern wall below the window, an analogical medieval portrayal of the donor, is covered with illusive embossment. The bronze group of statues of St. Agnes is the work of K. Stádník of 1989 The chapel has Late Renaissance tarsia pews of about 1610.

The basement of the cathedral

Access to the basement of the cathedral is gained by means of a flight of steps running from the Chapel of the Holy Rood. A sightseeing tour takes us first to a part of the eastern crypt (the crypt of SS. Cosma and Damian) of St. Vitus's Basilica of Prince Spytihněv II of after 1060. The peripheral masonry of the apse, whose interior is broken up by recesses, has been preserved as have the columns decorated with capitals which bore the vault of the crypt. A part of the altar table as well as a part of the original cretaceous marly limestone paving have also been preserved. A casting of the remainders of a medieval grave of priests is situated on the left side. In the corner a narrow passage closed with a grille turns to the left. Beyond the grille is the inaccessible area of excavations below St. Wenceslas's Chapel with the masonry of the southern apse of the Wenceslas Rotunda (of the first third of the 10th centry). In the narrow passage leading to the Royal Tomb remainders of the masonry of the northern apse of the rotunda can be seen beyond the grille.

The Royal Tomb. This tomb was built-in into the remainders of the former so-called monastery of the Church of Prague, i.e., the seat of the St. Vitus chapter, in the late 16th century. Visible in front of the tomb, on the right side, is the peripheral masonry of the basilica, while on the left side the courtyard wall of the apse with one of the feet for the

ROYAL TOMB

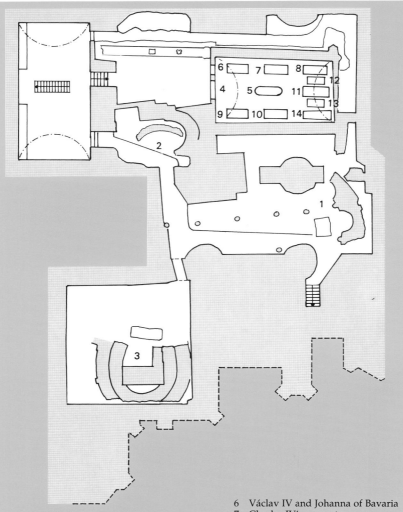

THE BASEMENT OF THE CATHEDRAL

1. Eastern crypt of the Basilica of SS. Vitus, Wenceslas and Adalbert
2. Remainder of the northern apse of St. Vitus's Rotunda
3. Southern apse of the rotunda
4. Royal tomb
5. Charles IV
6. Václav IV and Johanna of Bavaria
7. Charles IV's consorts
8. Jan Zhořelecký and an unknown person
9. Ladislav Pohrobek
10. George of Poděbrady
11. Rudolph II
12. Václav, son of Charles IV
13. Eleonora, Rudolph I called Gruel and Duke Rudolph
14. Marie Amálie

columns of the wide windows can be seen. The tomb itself is a small cellar with a barrel vault. In the years 1928 to 1935 it was subjected to adaptations carried out by the architect K. Roškot. These included a design of new sarcophagi in which the bodily remains of Czech kings and other members of the ruling families (with the exception of Rudolph II and the Grandduchess Maria Amelia of Parma) were laid. Charles IV (†1378) lays at rest in the position of honour in the centre, while standing behind one another on the right side are the tombs of Ladislav Pohrobek (†1457), Václav IV (†1419) and his consort Johana of Bavaria and the original tin coffin of Maria Amelia (daughter of Maria Theresa) (†1804). The tombs of George of Poděbrady (†1471), the consorts and children of Charles IV, Jan Zhořelecký (†1396) and unknown persons are situated by the left wall. In the centre at the rear is the original tin coffin containing the bodily remains of Rudolph II (†1612). Let into the floor on both sides are two caskets: the one on the left holds the remains of Václav, Charles IV's underage son, and the one on the right those of the Czech king Rudolph I called Gruel (†1307) and Eleonora, daughter of Maxmilián II (†1580).

The entrance area from the Royal Tomb is occupied by a <u>collection of sculpture,</u> supplemented with the sculpted ground-plans of the masonry of the rotunda and basilica, realized according to the results of K. Hilbert's research.

RUDOLPH II'S COFFIN

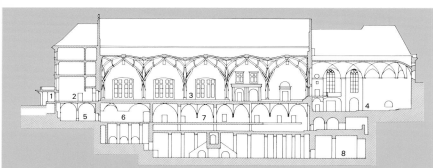

LONGITUDINAL SECTION OF THE PALACE
1. Entrance from the Third Courtyard
2. Antechamber
3. Vladislav Hall
4. All Saints' Church
5. Václav IV's Hall of Columns
6. Old Registry
7. Charles's room
8. Romanesque floor, interior below Romanesque All Saints' Chapel

THE OLD ROYAL PALACE
Architectural development

The eastern side of the Third Courtyard is closed by the Old Royal Palace. Below Pacassi's façade of the time of its Theresian reconstruction it practically does not differ outwardly from the other palace wings of Prague Castle. However, in actual fact it is an intricate complex of buildings which gradually grew and changed throughout a whole millennium until it gained its present appearance.

The site of the present palace was formerly occupied by the original seat of Czech princes of the late 9th century. It was unquestionably mainly built of wood even though it was probably soon replaced by a masonry-built residence. The oldest palace was later covered by other buildings and so we shall evidently not get to know more about it.

The later Romanesque princes' palace, built during the reign of Soběslav II in the course of the wide-scale reconstruction of the

The palace was subjected to a big reconstruction after 1333, after the return of the later emperor and king Charles IV from France. As the foundation for his seat Charles IV used the preserved lower part of the Romanesque building, but widened it with a band of arcades. In this way he gained greater space also for a reception hall on the upper floor and simultaneously determined the present width of the palace. In the given period he also widened the royal seat in westerly direction, where he also included the tower of the Romanesque fortifications, which had stood separately till then, with the former southern gate.

During the reign of Václav IV two perpendicular wings were built and some interiors were provided with new vaults. A new church, consecrated to All Saints and inspired by the magnificent Sainte-Chapelle in Paris, originated at the same time.

After Václav IV moved to the Royal Court in the Old Town the palace remained deserted for a whole century. It was finally Vladislav Jagiello, who returned here after 1483, that commenced its new reconstruction. A small audience hall clearly originated first, whereupon a big hall of ceremonies began to develop which still bears the name of its founder. The bold vault of the hall, which has no inner supports, is the work of Benedikt Ried similarly as the perpendicular palace wing named after Vladislav's son and successor Ludvík.

After the catastrophic fire of 1541 the Diet and All Saints' Church had to be rebuilt. The wing of the New Land Rolls was enlarged at the same time.

In the 18th century the palace was subjected to several utilitarian interventions. In this respect special mention can be made of the extension of the Theresian Wing in front of the southern façade.

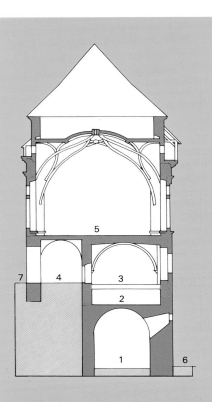

**CROSS-SECTION
OF THE OLD ROYAL PALACE**

1 Roman floor
2 Lowered Gothic floor
3 Charles's room
4 Arcade
5 Vladislav Hall
6 Southern courtyard
7 Northern courtyard
Green = Romanesque,
Red = Gothic,
Blue = Late Gothic masonry

Castle after 1135, has been preserved in a considerably better if not complete state. On its eastern side the long building of a rectangular ground-plan was protected by a fortification wall. It was also fortified with pentagonal turrets. All Saints' Chapel, consecrated in 1185, connected up with the palace on its eastern side.

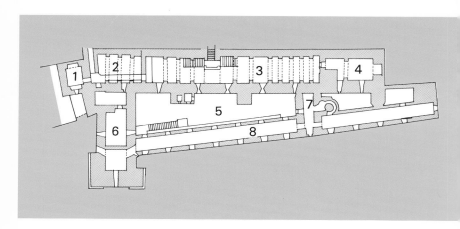

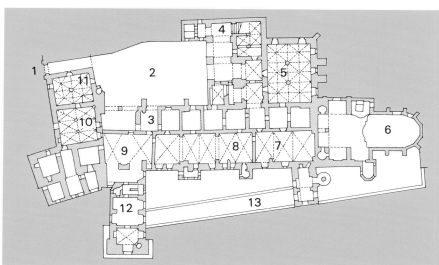

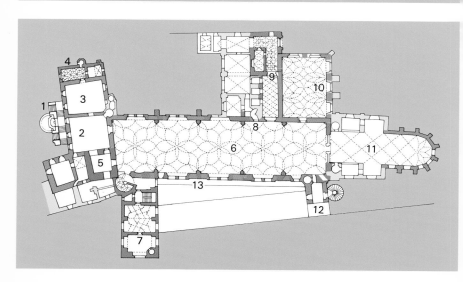

THE OLD ROYAL PALACE
Individual parts
The Romanesque underground part
The entrance to the oldest part of the palace. Access to the Romanesque underground part of the palace is gained by means of a <u>flight of steps from the western open arcade and from</u> the area below the <u>Riders' Staircase.</u> The palace is divided into four areas on this level (in the second basement):

The former passageway of the southern gate. The first area is the site where, after 1135, a tower-like gate, built as a part of the castle fortifications some distance from the palace in westerly direction, stood.

The area with the remainders of a mound. It is possible to cross this area by means of a wooden footbridge affording a view of the remainders of the original fortifications of the Castle. Its earth mound was fortified inside by a wooden structure and on the outside by a stone wall built with the use of the dry method, without mortar.

BELOW ALL SAINTS' CHAPEL
ON THE ROMANESQUE FLOOR

ROMANESQUE GROUND-FLOOR OF THE PALACE

The former ground-floor of the palace. The third area represents the former ground-floor of the palace, built at the same time as the fortification wall after 1135. The present large <u>hall</u> was, however, <u>originally divided into smaller rooms.</u>

The barrel <u>vault,</u> strengthened with several bands of vaults of hewn stone, is <u>Romanesque.</u> The vaults were additionally strengthened with bands of bricks during the recon-struction of the palace in the Gothic period.

The use of the Romanesque storeys. It is not possible to say anything defin-ite about the use of these parts. These parts could have served, as was usual at castles, as storerooms for a large number of people. In later times wine cellars originated here and in 1547, after the unsuccessful uprising against Ferdinand I, burghers were imprisoned here, among them also

SOUTHERN COURTYARD

Bishop Jan Augusta of the Czech Brethren.

The lower storey of the Romanesque chapel. The semicircular vaulted portal affords access to the square interior – the lower storey of the Romanesque chapel consecrated to All Saints. On the right of the entrance there is a huge block of masonry which differs clearly from the rest of the masonry of Romanesque ashlars. This block forms the base of the staircase of the 16th century. At the end of World War II the Czech coronation jewels were walled-up in a special cellar.

CHARLES'S ROOM

The Gothic storey

The arcades of the time of Charles IV. The Gothic storey (the first basement of the contemporary palace) spreads out on the level of the northern palace courtyard and below it there are again remainders of masonry unearthed in the course of archeological research and covered with a reinforced ceiling in 1946. Opening into the courtyard with pointed arches are three of the ten arcades which Charles IV had built to widen the too narrow palace in northerly direction. During the reign of Václav IV all the arcades were walled-up and remained so apart from the mentioned three. These were rid of their brickwork as late as after 1930.

The Room of the Old Land Rolls. Entrance to this room is gained from the area below the Riders' Staircase by passing through a Renaissance portal with twisted columns. The effective heavy vault of the large room rests on two low round columns. (One of them had to be changed in 1990 due to the bad state it was in. In the course of this work the vault was supported by a well-built wooden structure.) The name of the room betrays the fact that it served as a safe for the land rolls, i.e., the books containing records of the decisions of the provincial court and with records of the maintenance of the property of the nobility. Their

VÁCLAV IV'S HALL OF COLUMNS

destruction during the fire of 1541 meant an immense loss for the whole kingdom.

A number of remarkable sights. One of the fields of the arcade passage passes into a room with a rib vault. In the course of adaptations carried out in the Thirties of the present century it was rid of its floor in order that the remainders of a living-room with a corner fireplace, dating in the Romanesque period, might be visible. Here attention is also deserved by the façade wall of the palace chapel consecrated to All Saints with two portals situated above each other and with the print of a staircase leading to the upper portal to the tribune of the princes. On the opposite side, between the footbridge and the transverse wall, preserved remainders of a furnace for hot-air heating, evidently of the 15th century, can be seen. This system of heating was known already in medieval Rome. The fire in the furnace heated a layer of big stones laid on bands of bricks. These hot stones then heated the air which flowed over them and was immediately carried by channels in the masonry to other rooms.

Charles's Room. The neighbouring room originated as the result of the connecting-up of three original interiors. At their time, during the reign of Charles IV, they had flat ceilings. Their rib vaults date from the time of the reconstruction of the time of the Václav IV. The additionally built vault made it necessary to shift some of the windows and also conditioned the realization of another big move: during the lowering of the rooms the floors were also lowered with the result that the lower floor on a Romanesque vault became unusable and was filled in. Passing through the room, by the southern peripheral wall, are huge pillars which on the floor above bear the vault of the Vladislav Hall. The original division into three rooms is indicated by big brick arches and also by bands in the paving, which originated in the Thirties of the present century after found Gothic tiles with a stylized leaf and, on the small area of a recess, also with the Czech lion and the imperial eagle. The last field of the vault of Charles's Room was provided with graffito decoration in the 16th century.

The Old Registry. The Czech Chamber kept its accounts in the next room. Its area was extended during the adding of the Ludvík Wing in the early 16th century. The pillar with the remainder of a big fireplace stands separately, precisely below another fireplace in the Vladislav Hall situated one floor higher. According to the cretaceous marly limestone ashlars, burned to a red colour, in the western wall of the room it is possible to recognize the masonry of the Romanesque southern tower. Next to it is a passage leading to the Hall of Columns – the most remarkable interior on the Gothic floor.

The Hall of Columns of Václav IV. This hall originated about 1400 and ranks among the last buildings to be completed at Prague Castle before the outbreak of the Hussite wars. The interior of the hall is the work of the royal building workshop, which also built Točník Castle, of which Václav was very fond.

SO-CALLED
VLADISLAV'S BEDCHAMBER ▶

The Chamber of the Court Rolls.

From the Hall of Columns it is possible to ascend several steps and enter another room with a <u>Renaissance vault</u> on a central pillar. It served as the depository of the Court Rolls, an institution similar to the

EMBLEMS IN THE VLADISLAV HALL

DETAIL
OF VLADISLAV'S BEDCHAMBER

Land Rolls, but attached to the Court of Justice of the royal court.

The representation floor

The entrance part. The main entrance to the Old Royal Palace leads from the Third Courtyard directly to the representative floor. The first two rooms, the <u>antechamber and the Green Chamber,</u> were <u>rid of their Late Gothic vaults during adaptations carried out in the 18th century.</u>

The present antechamber was originally a small room which later, from the succession of Ferdinand I to the throne up to the mid-18th century, served as the Czech Chamber. The ashlar masonry, reddened by fire, once again belongs to the Romanesque southern tower. The <u>two arches</u> by the entrance to the Vladislav Hall <u>bear a part of the passage leading to the Royal Oratory of St. Vitus's Cathedral.</u> During the reign of Maria Theresa this passage was extended.

The Green Chamber. This chamber was originally an assembly hall for minor court sessions. From 1512 it served the purposes of the court and chamber courts. Its <u>walls are decorated with the coats-of-arms of the clerks of the chamber court</u> of the 18th century. The <u>fragments of provincial emblems</u> (of the Czech Kingdom and Upper and Lower Lusatia) have been preserved on the walls perhaps from the time of Ferdinand I, when this room served as an assembly hall. During assemblies of

VLADISLAV HALL

DETAIL OF ENTRANCE
TO THE VLADISLAV HALL

emphasized with gilded stylized leaves. On the coping stones there are the provincial emblems (Bohemia, Moravia, Silesia, Luxembourg) and on their fronts the king's monogram (W-Wladislav) and the crowned Polish female eagle. (The fact that the Hungarian emblem is missing among the others dates the origin of the room before 1490, when Vladislav became king of Hungary.) The walls of the audience hall are decorated with the painted coats-of-arms of the supreme controllers of the household of the 16th century.

The Vladislav Hall

The central interior of the whole floor is the Vladislav Hall, at its time the biggest secular vaulted hall in Central Europe. The royal architect Benedikt Ried built it with the use of the peripheral walls of Charles IV's palace, However, he demolished the transverse dividing wall and all the older orifices. He based the five fields of the curved rib vault on huge pillars, which by the walls pass through the two lower floors. Running from the pillars in a fan-like manner are the ribs of the vault, forming a six-petalled rose in the centre of each field.

The eastern front of the hall bears the date 1500. The numbers by the emblem of the Czech and Hungarian Kingdom indicate that in the year of the completion of the vault Vladislav Jagiello had been the Czech king for twenty-nine years and the Hungarian king for ten years. In the southern and northern walls there are unusually big windows, the first manifestation of the Renaissance style at Prague Castle. The large hall was originally heated by two fireplaces. The wooden floor most likely dates from the time of the coronation of Leopold II (1791). Three of the tin chandeliers are originals of the 16th century, the other two being modern replicas.

The Vladislav Hall served mainly for royal representation. Coronation festivities, banquets and ceremonies during which homage was paid to the sovereign were held here. Sessions of the Diet also took place here, apart from others also the St. Bartholomew Diet (1547) at which

the Provincial Diet members of the knightage used the Green Chamber for meetings. This chamber is inscribed in history also due to the fact that before the defenestration on 23 May, 1618 representatives of the non-Catholic estates gathered here. – The Baroque fresco on the ceiling (The Trial of Solomon) was transferred here from the courtroom of the Burgrave's Office in 1963.

The small audience hall. Two smaller rooms are accessible from the Green Chamber. The first of them is traditionally incorrectly referred to as Vladislav's Bedchamber. It really did originate during the reign of Vladislav Jagiello, but it served as a small audience hall. The importance of this room is stressed by the decorative, Late Gothic vault with polychromed ribs whose intersecting places are

Ferdinand I strictly limited the provincial rights and privileges of the Estates after the unsuccessful uprising of the nobility and towns. For tournaments of knights the participants entered the Vladislav Hall by means of the Riders' Staircase. When the court met with diplomats and invited guests at Rudolph II's time ladies and gentlemen promenaded and conversed here, enjoyed the view of the town and selected luxurious goods offered by merchants on stalls situated directly in the hall.

On the occasion of certain ceremonies the vault of the hall was adorned with a decorative painting. The last of these works, painted by Josef Navrátil in 1836, was removed during the renewal of the hall in 1928.

The tradition of the Vladislav Hall as the scene of important political events was accepted also by the First Republic. In 1934 T. G. Masaryk was elected president of the Republic for the third time and other presidential elections have also taken place in this historic environment.

TERRACE OF THE THERESIAN WING

The Ludvík Wing
Access to the Ludwík Wing is gained through a portal in the south-western core of the Vladislav Hall (next to the fireplace of the past).

The Rooms of the Czech Office. The two rooms of the Czech Office are situated in the Ludvík Wing on the level of the Vladislav Hall. In the case of the absence of the sovereign the Office was the supreme administrative organ in the country. The first room has a rib vault with remarkable consoles. The second, which is entered through a portal with the crowned initial L (Ludvík Jagellio), has a vault whose ribs have been cut away. It was from the window in the eastern wall of this room that, on 23 May, 1618, two of the governors, Jaroslav Bořita of Martinic and Smečno and Vilém Slavata of Chlum and Košumberk along with the secretary Filip Fabricius, were thrown. This event ignited the uprising of the Czech Estates and the Thirty Years War.

The office of the Imperial Court Council. A spiral staircase makes it possible to ascend to the next floor and enter the room used by the Imperial Court Council at the time of Rudolph II. The interior is purely Renaissance and is illuminated by big windows. It has office furniture of the 17th century and a big tiled stove

SPIRAL STAIRCASE AT THE ENTRANCE TO THE LUDVÍK WING

LENGTH OF HALL 62 m, WIDTH 16 m
◀ AND HEIGHT 13 m

CZECH OFFICE

dating in the same period. The portraits on the walls are of the Czech kings of the Hapsburg dynasty. Twenty-seven of the participants in the uprising of the Estates were informed that the death sentence had been passed on them in the office of the Imperial Court Council, directly above the room from which the defenestration took place. The condemned persons were executed in Old Town Square on 21 June 1621.

Observation places
In the southern wall of the Vladislav Hall there are two ways of access to an observation gallery, reconstructed during the First Republic and made newly accessible in 1993.The gallery affords a fine view of the city and of

PORTAL OF THE CZECH OFFICE

DEFENESTRATION WINDOW

the Garden on the Ramparts, where sandstone obelisks mark the places where the two governors fell during the defenestration in 1618. A good view of the façade of the Ludvík Wing (the first façade of pure Renaissance design in Bohemia) and details of the Early Renaissance windows of the Vladislav Hall can be obtained as well.

The last entrance in the southern wall affords access to a a small observation terrace, built on the demolished part of the wing at the time of Václav IV. Next to the terrace there is an open spiral staircase built of granite. It is a remarkable work of the architect Otto Rothmayer and forms a connection between the Old Royal Palace and the Theresian Wing.

The Theresian Wing

Maria Theresa had this narrow tract built in the years 1766 to 1766 as a connection between the Ludvík Wing and the Institute of Gentlewomen. The lower floors were occupied by offices, registries and flats, while the top floor (no longer in existence) served as a connecting passage. When the clerks employed in the offices situated at that time on the Gothic floor of the Old Palace complained that after the construction of the wing they would not have sufficient light for their work the head of the building office replied at great length that the building was being erected on the basis of an order issued by the empress, that the distance between the building and the windows of the offices was adequate and that the fact that they would not have a view of the town should only double their work endeavours. In 1931 the highest floor of the Theresian Wing was removed for the opposite reason: in order that it might not prevent a view from the town of the façade of the Vladislav Hall. In 1937 Otto Rothmayer began to carry out modifications which could not, however, be completed until 1952. After the last construction, finished in 1993, the Theresian Wing was made available for exhibition purposes.

The wing of the New Land Rolls and the Diet

There are three portals in the northern wall of the Vladislav Hall. They lead to the offices of the New Land Rolls, to the Diet and to the Riders' Staircase.

The offices of the New Land Rolls.

These are reached by means of a spiral staircase. The four rooms concerned served as the offices and depository of the clerks of the New Land Rolls from the Sixties of the 16th century. Their walls and vaults are decorated with the coats-of-arms of the supreme clerks of the kingdom and those of the Land Rolls from the 16th to the 18th century. An inscription on the western wall brings to mind the fact that "Nothing will be read to or written for anyone until payment is made in cash". The furniture is arranged according to the preserved order of the 18th century. Original carved cabinets of the time of Rudolph II stand in one of the rooms. Copies of books, so-called quires, are arranged in them. The

IMPERIAL OFFICE

"NOTHING WILL BE READ OR WRITTEN FOR ANYONE . . ."

individual volumes of the land books were originally differentiated by a characteristic, a colour and a painted sign on their back. Later use was made of numbers. In another room the oldest <u>piece of furniture of Prague Castle</u> – a Renaissance cabinet made of soft wood with surface carving and the date 1562 – has been preserved.

INTERIOR OF THE DIET

PAINTINGS IN A ROOM
◄ OF THE NEW LAND ROLLS

Adjoining the rooms of the New Land Rolls is a Baroque annex built by K. I. Dienzenhofer in 1737. It is not accessible to the public. Originally the directorate of the Office of the Land Rolls assembled here. In the 19th century the room served as a safe depository for the Crown Archives. The most important documents of the Czech Kingdom were accumulated here and in the years 1867 to 1868 the Czech crown jewels was also kept here.

The Diet. The Diet is situated in the perpendicular northern wing of the time of Václav IV. In the Jagiello period it was rebuilt by B. Ried, but in 1541 it was wholly destroyed by fire apart from the peripheral masonry. For its restoration two projects were available after the mid-16th century. Italian artists proposed a flat-ceilinged room of a Renaissance character, while Bonifaz Wolmut came forward with a pseudo-historic design. And the ruler decided in favour of the latter. True, from the formal aspect its <u>rib vault formally approximates the Diet to the neighbouring Vladislav Hall,</u> but it is a decoration rather than a structural element. The ribs, running from purely Renaissance pillasters, are broken up in places or freely hung below the vault.

The <u>tribune of the supreme scribe</u> on the contrary, features a purely Renaissance style. It was connected

THE OLDEST CABINET

with the rooms of the New Land Rolls – and this was very useful: during court assemblies in the Diet the scribe could easily find the required quire and immediately quote from it.

COATS-OF-ARMS OF CLERKS
IN A ROOM
OF THE NEW LAND ROLLS

The location of the furniture in the Diet recalls the assembly of the Provincial Diet after the issuing of the New Provincial Constitution in 1627. The throne with the Czech lion was intended for the king, the armchair on the right being occupied by the archbishop and the benches behind him by members of the clergy. The benches in front of the throne were reserved for lords and knights. Representatives of royal towns, who had only one vote among them in the Diet, stood on the gallery by the window. The supreme provincial clerks and judges sat on chairs and benches along the walls. The portraits in the Diet show Maria Theresa, her consort Franz Stephen of Lotharingia, Joseph II, Leopold II and Franz II. The tiled stove in Neo-Gothic style, the only one at Prague Castle, dates in 1836.

The Riders' Staircase. The area by means of which we now leave the Vladislav Hall was originally intended for the entry of knights on horseback who took part in the tournaments organized here. The remainder of the profiled Gothic portal proves that the main entrance was already here at Charles IV's time. From the former open loggia, later rebuilt and provided with a crest vault, we pass through a portal in the shape of an ass's back and come to the staircase proper with wide, low steps. This space was roofed by B. Ried with a complicated curved rib vault with intertwining ribs.

All Saints' Church
After 1370 Peter Parler built a church, consecrated to All Saints, on the site of the Romanesque palace chapel of the 12th century, likewise consecrated to All Saints. The new building had a higher vault and bigger tracery windows. Remainders of the vaults and traceries have been preserved in the attic. The windows can be seen from outside. According to old descriptions the church was magnificently decorated. However, after the fire of 1541 only its peripheral walls remained. It was not renewed until 1580, the costs incurred being paid by Rudolph II's sister, Queen Elizabeth, widow of the French king Charles IX.

RIDERS' STAIRCASE ▶

At that time the church was simultaneously extended to the façade of the
Vladislav Hall. It was provided with
a lower Renaissance vault with
plastic stucco ribs and smaller windows with pseudo-Gothic traceries.
Shortly before 1600 a portal with the
emblem of the Czech lion on the
gable extension, the work of Giovanni Gargiolli of Italy, was built in the
eastern wall of the Vladislav Hall. It
connects the Vladislav Hall with the
empora of All Saints' Church. After
1755 the church began to be used as
the chapel of the newly built Institute
of Gentlewomen.

The high altar is a Baroque work
with a painting All Saints of 1732,
realized by V. V. Reiner.

The cycle of paintings – the work of
Kristián Dittman of 1669 – portrays
twelve scenes from the legend about

ALL SAINTS' CHURCH

the fact that it is a replica of the work
of F. Salviati from St. Celestine's
Church in Paris it can be presumed
that it was also a gift from Queen
Elizabeth.

Standing in a recess on the northern
side of the nave is the Baroque
tomb of St. Procopius. Its carving is
attributed to F. I. Weiss. The tomb
with the figure of the saint is surrounded by allegorical sculptures of
the virtues and it is decorated with
reliefs from the legend about St.
Procopius. This tomb originally stood
in the centre of the choir, but in the
18th century it was moved, because it
obstructed the view of the inhabitants
of the Institute of Gentlewomen of
the altar. In the course of later
modifications in the years 1952 to
1953 the recess containing the tomb
was closed with a Baroque forged
grille, which had formerly separated
the presbytery from the nave. In the
period of from 1987 to 1988 restorers
removed the younger over-painting
and renewed the original gilding.

Since 1964 an organ built in Baroque
Gothic style has been installed on the
northern part of the choir. It was
brought here from the church at.
Skapce near Kladruby. Below the
choir on the southern side is the altar

PORTAL OF ALL SAINTS' CHURCH

St. Procopius. The last painting
depicts the solemn transfer of the
bodily remains of St. Procopius from
Sázava Monastery to All Saints'
Church in 1588. In the procession
behind the coffin of the saint the
Emperor Rudolph II can also be seen
walking with a lit candle.
Set in the Baroque architecture of the
right-hand side altar is a painting The
Removal from the Cross. In view of

ST. PROCOPIUS'S TOMBSTONE

ST. GEORGE'S BASILICA WITH THE FORMER CONVENT OF THE BENE-DICTINE NUNS

Architectural development

St. George's Basilica originated as the second church at Prague Castle and underwent a very complicated process of development. Nothing has been preserved above ground of the original building founded by Prince Vratislav about 920. At the time of the founding of the convent in 973 the church was enlarged and rebuilt. Other important changes came about after a fire which occurred in 1142. The renewed church was extended in westerly direction and in essence acquired its present appearance, the choir with the main apse and the two steeples. The southern one of these was built on to the chapel, which had previously stood separately. In the first half of the 13th century St. Ludmila's Chapel originated in addition to an entrance porticus on the western side. After the mid-14th century a new façade came into being in its place. In the Early Baroque period the church got its present

of the Holy Archangels. The triptych is attributed to the Rudolphian painter Hans von Aachen and dates in the late 16th century.

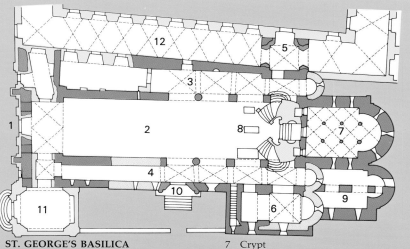

ST. GEORGE'S BASILICA
1 Western entrance
2 Main nave
3 Northern side aisle
4 Southern side aisle
5 Northern steeple
6 Southern steeple, Chapel of Our Lady
7 Crypt
8 Graves of Přemyslid princes
9 St. Ludmila's Chapel
10 Southern portal
11 St. John Nepomuk's Chapel
12 Southern branch of the cloister of the monastery

Grey = 10th century, Green = Romanesque, Red = Gothic, Blue = Renaissance, Yellow = Baroque masonry

EASTERN PART OF THE CASTLE

conspicuous façade and the monastery as a whole was in essence newly built. The Chapel of St. John Nepomuk was built from 1718 to 1722 by F. M. Kaňka. At Joseph II's time the abolished monastery was used by the army. In the years 1887 to 1908 the considerably delapidated church was restored after a design by F. Machek, who tried to restore its original Romanesque character. In 1958 to 1964 the church and the Court of Paradise of the monastery were subjected to archeological research and finally, from 1969 to 1975, the

monastery underwent reconstruction for the purpose of the installation of the exposition of Old Czech art of the National Gallery.

The exterior of the basilica

The western façade of the basilica. The brick-red colour of the building was typical of the Early Baroque. Its façade is broken up by pillasters. The corner pillasters terminate with slender obelisks, while the others are topped with sandstone statues portraying the founder of the church, Vratislav I. and the founder of the convent, the Blessed Mlada. The triangular gable is decorated with a stucco relief of St. George battling with the dragon. The twin steeples stand out well in the western façade although they are situated far to the east. The symmetry of the church is disturbed only by the attached Chapel of St. John Nepomuk, represented by a statue on the undulating cornice of the entrance portal.

INTERIOR OF ST. GEORGE'S BASILICA

The interior of the basilica

General view. The interior of the church has an austere Romanesque, but monumental character. At the time of Machek's restoration the main nave was provided with a beam ceiling in place of the removed vault. It is separated from the narrow side aisles by a wall broken up by an arcade in which a column and two pillars alternate. On the floors above the side aisles there are tribunes connected with the main nave by a row of dual windows.

The main nave. Hanging on the southern wall of the main nave is a large multipart painting with the central theme The Martyrdom of St. Ursula and 11,000 Christian Virgins by H. Burgkmair of the 16th century. On the opposite wall there is a painting The Assumption of Our Lady by J. J. Heintsch of the end or the 17th century. In the eastern part three tombstones indicate the place of burial of members of the Přemyslid family of princes, discovered in the course of archeological research. Standing on the right is a cretaceous marly limestone tomb with a wooden, house-like casket of the 15th century. The tomb contains the bodily remains of the founder of the church, Vratislav I († 921). Painted on the eastern front of the casket is Prince Vratislav with a model of the basilica and portrayed on the opposite front is the Abbess Mlada handing a crosier to Dětmar, the first archbishop of Prague. The tomb in the centre bears the original tombstone of red sandstone. Below it archeologists unearthed an undisturbed grave with the imprint of a coffin hollowed out from a tree trunk. According to the archeologist I. Borkovský they are those of Prince Boleslav II. († 999), while the more recent research of the anthropologist E. Vlček attributes them to Prince Oldřich († 1034). The grave on the left is a modern one for the bodily remains of other members of the family of princes.

CZECH LION ON TOMB OF VRATISLAV I

VIEW OF THE INTERIOR OF THE CRYPT

PAINTINGS ON THE VAULT

The choir and the crypt in the choir.
Behind the gravestones a symmetrical Baroque staircase leads to the square choir, below which the eastern crypt has been preserved. It is roofed with a system of cross vaults borne by columns with cubic capitals. Standing <u>on the altar table</u> in the axis of the crypt is the <u>casting of a Romanesque tympanum with The Enthroned Madonna with Angels</u>. Portrayed in the relief as donors are the abbesses Mlada, Berta and Anežka and her brother, King Přemysl Otakar I. <u>On the table by the eastern wall of the crypt there is a stone allegory of Vanity,</u> a naturalistic portrayal of a human body in a state of decomposition with snakes and lizards in its entrails. A legend has it that the statue was sculptured by the Italian stonemason Spinetti in the 18th century as a penance for the murder of his beloved. However, the sculpture is evidently two hundred years older.

<u>Preserved on the vault of the choir are the remainders of a wall painting</u> Heavenly Jerusalem of the <u>early 13th century</u> and to be seen in the apse is now only a part of the painting The Coronation of Our Lady of the late

SOUTHERN PORTAL OF THE BASILIKA

ST. LUDMILA'S CHAPEL

16th century. In the northern wall of the choir there is a small portal decorated with so-called berries on the jamb and a Renaissance sandstone sanctuarium.

St. Ludmila's Chapel. The choir is adjoined on the southern side by St. Ludmila's Chapel, separated by a Baroque marble balustrade with a forged grille. <u>Wall paintings of the late 16th century</u> have been preserved on the <u>vault,</u> which was renewed after the fire of 1541. They represent the Virgin Mary, Christ, the four evangelists and the Czech provincial saints. <u>St. Ludmila is painted</u>

on the arch of triumph. Princess Ludmila's tomb stands in the centre of the chapel. It is composed of parts whose ages differ. The upper slab with the figure of the saint and the side panels with small reliefs of saints date in the 14th century, the supplements, including the iron grille, having originated in 1858.

The northern side aisle. A semicircular vaulted portal leads from the northern side aisle to the cloister of the convent. Its vaulted arch is decorated with ornamental painting of the 13th century. Fragments of wall paintings can be seen in the apse, which dates in the 10th century. The torso of a pieta stands on the altar table. It was hewn from cretaceous marly limestone and polychromed and is most likely the work of the Parler workshop of the latter half of the 14th century.

The southern side aisle. This aisle is used for a small exposition of the results of the archeological and anthropological research of the basilica, the convent and the graves unearthed here. The tombstones of several abbesses of St. George's Convent are set in the southern wall. A wooden Late Gothic statue of St.

Bartholomew stands in the apse which, similarly as the northern one, is one of the oldest preserved parts of the church. Adjoining the side aisle in front of the apse is the area below the southern steeple, originally the separate Chapel of Our Lady. The original grave of St. Ludmila was most likely situated here. Fragments of the wall paintings have been preserved, these being somewhat younger than the paintings in the choir. Originally they passed over the brickwork of the window of the apse, abolished after the building-on of St. Ludmila's Chapel at the time of the abbess Anežka, i.e., in the years 1200 to 1228. On the vault can again be seen a composition Heavenly Jerusalem and on the conch of the apse there is a painting Maiestas Domini (Enthroned Christ in an aureole with angels and apostles). A panel on the wall shows the ground-plan of the building with indication of the individual building phases and on display in a cabinet is a plaster casting of the statue of St. Ludmila from the saint's tomb. The altar table is decorated with an original Late Gothic relief The Adoration of the Three Kings, hewn from cretaceous marly limestone and polychromed.

EXPOSITION OF THE BAROQUE IN THE CONVENT

An Early Renaissance portal, the work of B. Ried's workshop of about 1515, leads from the southern side sisle to Jiřská Street. It evidently stands on the site of an older Romanesque portal. The portal proper with smaller fluted half-columns and <u>with a relief of George battling with the dragon</u> is set in larger portal architecture of a similar scheme: fluted half-columns with vegetable capitals bear a lintel with a triangular gable. The slanting ceiling, divided up by casettes with stylized flowers, is a remarkable feature. (The relief of St. George here is a casting. The original can be seen in the exposition of the National Gallery in the convent.)

St. John Nepomuk's Chapel. The rectangular chapel consecrated to St. John Nepomuk adjoins the southern side aisle in the west. The apotheosis of this provincial saint in the cupola of the vault was painted by V. V. Reiner in 1722. The two altars are also decorated with paintings of the saint by V. V. Reiner, the painting of the Virgin Mary with the Child Jesus being the work of an unknown painter. Scenes from the life of St. John Nepomuk are also portrayed in the paintings on the walls. However, the cycle is incomplete.

St. George's Convent

<u>The convent is a large Early Baroque building of an austere appearance. It has a Court of Paradise and another inner courtyard.</u> The reinforced concrete structure covers the excavations below the Court of Paradise.

ST. GEORGE'S BASILICA

The present quadratura of the last quarter of the 17th century which surrounds the Court of Paradise has vaults decorated with a simple stucco ornament. One branch of the quadratura passes through the northern Romanesque steeple of the basilica. The passages of the steeple originated additionally and were vaulted in the 13th century. Fragments of wall paintings can also be seen here. The weakening of the masonry and its imperfect founding in the slanting ground resulted in the northern steeple beginning to lean dangerously to one side. Its technically complicated levelling and the securing of its static safety therefore formed parts of its last reconstruction.

From the eastern branch of the cloister access can be gained to the convent chapel consecrated to St. Anne, whose original decoration has been preserved. The foundations of a Romanesque chapel have been found below the paving. In the 14th century St. Anne's Chapel was rebuilt and enlarged (The pointed tracery window in the eastern wall has survived since that time.) The chapel underwent its last reconstruction in the late 17th century when the whole convent was changed.

What are presumed to be the remains of the abbess Mlada, dressed in a nun's robe and decorated with a silver mask, are placed in a glazed recess. They were removed from a grave in the 18th century, but according to the results of research they are much younger and cannot belong to the founder of the convent. The tomb of Abbess Kunhuta of the Přemyslid dynasty († 1321) is decorated with the engraved figure of the deceased in an architectural frame.

To be seen in the chapel are the St. George altar, a panel painting of the 15th century and an original three-part cretaceous marly limestone relief of the Madonna with donors of the first third of the 13th century.The crosier and crown of the abbesses of St. George's Convent are kept in a glazed cabinet. After the abolition of the convent these symbols were used by the abbesses of the Theresian Institute of Gentlewomen, to which the right to crown the Czech queens also passed.

SQUARES, STREETS, HOUSES
ST. GEORGE'S SQUARE

The square named after St. George spreads out beyond the east end of St. Vitus's Cathedral. In the early Middle Ages the centre of the Castle area was probably just here. According to written sources a stone throne stood here on which a newly elected prince was symbolically seated. As a rule the election of home rulers was not recognized without this procedure.

In the middle part of the square rocky outcrop protruded above the present level of the paving and sloped in both southern and northern direction. Thanks to archeological research carried out from 1984 to 1989 it is known that until the 12th century there were no buildings on the area of the present square, but later small masonry-built and wooden houses were erected along the path leading to the gate of the convent. St. Vitus's and St. George's Basilicas were connected by a vaulted passage. After these buildings had ceased to exist several bigger houses were built along the northern side of the square (at least one of them already in the 14th century). In the 16th century the square had a round fountain in its centre to which water was supplied by wooden piping.

Nowadays St. George's Square is lined in the north by Mocker's Houses. This collective name is used to denote the Neo-Gothic buildings of the New Deanery (No. 34), which projects to a greater extent into the square, and the two cannons' residences (Nos. 35 and 36), whose façade is on the level of the other buildings in Vikářská Street. They were built in the years 1879 to 1881 after a project of the architect J. Mocker on the site of demolished, mostly Renaissance houses. In the direction away from the convent these were: the house of the supreme scribe, the office of the captain, the St. Vitus presbytery and the one-time secret armoury. The abolition of so many historic buildings meant a great and irreplaceable loss for Prague Castle. However, the Neo-Gothic buildings, whose demolition was also considered in the past, are now of great value as historic monuments. The New Deanery, a wholly uniform building as regards style, beginning with its symmetrical façade with two gables and ending with details of its interior, is particularly remarkable.

The square is closed on its eastern side by the façade of the Basilica and Convent of St. George and in the south by several parts of the Old Royal Palace: the wing of the New Land Rolls, the Diet and All Saints' Church. The façade of the Old Royal Palace is Renaissance, but originally (until 1730) it had three conspicuous gables. The adjoining façade of All Saints' Church of about 1580 has a remarkable Renaissance portal with pseudo-Gothic traceries in the pointed windows. Outstanding right in the corner of the square is the round columned portico of the Institute of Gentlewomen.

JIŘSKÁ STREET

Jiřská Street runs from St. George's Square in the direction of the eastern gate of Prague Castle, passing the southern façade of the basilica with ashlar masonry of the 10th to the 12th century, its southern steeple and the thoroughly renewed part of the east end. The revealed Romanesque masonry of the convent chapel consecrated to St. Anne can also be seen over the enclosing wall.

The Institute of Gentlewomen. The opposite side of the street is formed by the long, broken façade of the Institute of Gentlewomen. Single houses began to originate on the site of the big architectural complex in the 13th and 14th centuries. In 1513 a part of the plot occupied by the later palace fell into the hands of the lords of Rožmberk. The destruction or considerable damage of all the local buildings during the fire of 1541 freed space for them for a new, magnificent building. First of all there originated, under the supervision of the architect Hans Vlach, a four-winged palace with two arcades in the two shorter wings and with a gate affording access to Jiřská Street. Later, when the Rožmberks had also gained the neighbouring houses of the lords of Švamberk and Rožmitál, they supplemented the palace on its western side with

a large garden lined with an arcaded gallery. The building works were headed by Ulrico Avostalis in the years 1573 to 1574. In 1600 Rudolph II acquired the palace on a barter basis and had it connected with the Ludvík Wing by means of a wooden passage on pillars. In the Twenties of the 18th century the palace was raised in height by the addition of two new floors and divided inside by means of partition walls (T. Haffenecker). From 1753 it was converted into the Institute for Gentlewomen (A. Luragho after a project by N. Pacassi). After 1918, when the institute was abolished, the palace was used by the Ministry of the Interior until quite recently. This explains why the whole building was one of the least accessible and the least scientifically studied buildings of the Castle. The present appearance of the Institute of Gentlewomen is, it is true, marked by certain utilitarian adaptations carried out after World War II, but in essence it corresponds to its state of the latter half of the 18th century. The columned entrance portico on a circular ground-plan by All Saints' Church is decorated with copies of the original sculptures by the court sculptor J. Klein. The green colour of the façade was renewed in accordance with the results of archival research and research of the façades in the early Eighties. The

CEILING ON THE FIRST
FLOOR OF LOBKOWICZ PALACE

rooms in the building are now used by the Office of the President of the Republic and the Administration of Prague Castle as offices.

Lobkowicz Palace. This palace with a simple, plain façade and with two inner courtyards neighbours with the former Institute of Gentlewomen. Thanks to archeological and architectural-historical research we also have

THE GREAT HALL

a relatively good idea of the development of this building. Small dwelling-houses originated on a free site already in the 13th century and later two big Gothic houses were built here and named after their owners – the House of Zikmund of Freygut and Kapliřovský House. It was not until before the mid-16th that the construction of the palace was started by Wolf Krajíř of Krajka and continued after him, from 1554, by the lords of Pernštejn. In the first Renaissance phase the palace had four wings round a courtyard and was richly decorated with architectural elements of burnt clay, which the Pernštejns used also on other buildings. In the course of the next two building phases the palace gained its present size. In the years 1651 to 1668 it was rebuilt by C. Luragho for Václav Eusebius of Lobkowicz in the somewhat austere Early Baroque style.
Inside the building, on the level of the

first floor, two interiors and a chapel have been preserved in their original form. They are decorated with rich stucco ceilings, the work of D. Galli, with painted fillings by F. V. Harovník. In the 19th century the great hall of a height of two floors and with wall paintings of the 17th century was divided by the insertion of a ceiling and partition walls. Finally it was renewed during the general reconstruction carried out from 1973 to 1986. Since then the palace has been used by the National Museum for its exposition devoted to old Czech history and for occasional exhibitions, lectures and concerts.

The Residence of the Supreme Burgrave. Standing opposite Lobkowicz Palace is a high wall broken up by a gate with four stone coats-of-arms. All of them belonged to Supreme Burgraves: Adam of Valdštejn (1636, on the left), Jaroslav Bořita of Martinic (1642, on the right), Jan Josef of Vrtba (1712, in the centre below) and Karel Egon of Fürstenberk (1780, in the centre above). The gate affords access to the enclosed area of the Residence of the Supreme Burgrave. It is presumed that the castellan of the Castle, from whose function the office of the Supreme Burgrave was gradually developed, resided just in this part of the Castle, at least from the Romanesque period. (The Supreme Burgrave was the highest

FROM THE EXPOSITION
OF THE NATIONAL MUSEUM

GATE TO THE BURGRAVE'S HOUSE

clerk in the kingdom and represented the ruler in his absence.) A part of the Romanesque tower built-on on to the fortification wall and preserved to the present in the building of the Burgrave's House is perhaps a remainder of the burgrave's dwelling of the distant past. In the 14th century the house of the burgrave was certainly considerably big and comfortable, because for quite some time it served as the residence of the next king and emperor Charles IV. In 1541 it was destroyed by fire and fourteen years later it was rebuilt in Renaissance style by the Italian architect G. Ventura. In the years 1961 to 1963 the whole area was reconstructed after a project by J. Hlavatý in order to meet the needs of the House of Czechoslovak Children. In the course of this work some buildings were demolished and replaced with new ones (the entrance wing and the atrium). The two-storeyed main building of the Burgrave's House has renewed Renaissance gables on its shorter sides. A slender staircase tower is connected with the building practically in the centre of its southern façade. The graffito on all the façades was renewed for the first time in 1925 and then again during the reconstruction realized in the early Sixties.

The original ground-plan is still clearly perceptible in the interior of the building. The ground-floor was divided into four parts with barrel vaults: the lower part of a Romanesque tower, discovered by K. Fiala in 1932, has been preserved in the easternmost of them. On the first floor there are two interiors with Renaissance crest vaults and a court of justice approximately in the centre of the whole ground-plan. The richly painted beam ceiling in the court of justice has been cleaned and restored in Renaissance style. The ceiling was covered with a Baroque soffit with a painting The Judgement of Solomon. In 1963 this was removed and newly situated in the Green Chamber of the Old Royal Palace.

THE SUPREME BURGRAVE'S RESIDENCE

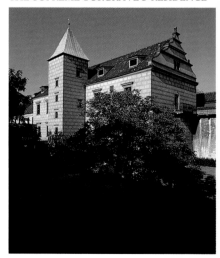

CEILING OF THE COURTROOM

Renaissance painted allegories of the senses and the elements (the models for them were Sadeler's engravings after drawings by Marten de Vos) and another painting with the theme The Judgement of Solomon have been preserved on the walls. Similarly as in other official interiors here, too, there is a cartouche with the inscription "Nothing will be read or written for anyone before being paid for in cash". The ornamental painting of the hangings with a pomegranate motif has been newly supplemented to a great extent.

During the reconstruction process two houses were also joined to the Burgrave's House: house No. 11 in the Golden Lane and No. 7 (the so-called Small Lobkowicz Palace) in the western part of the area.

The decoration of the interiors was influenced to a considerable degree by the politically tinged requirements of various art committees of the Sixties. The then political practice also left its mark on the statue Youth in front of the Burgrave's House (M. Zet, 1963), which definitely does not rank among opportunistic works. In accordance with the decision of the organs concerned this statue of a nude youth was rid of the genitals and only after the shame which marked the unveiling ceremony was its original appearance restored on the basis of an order issued by President Novotný.

The Black Tower. This tower to which a house, adapted to serve as the office of the House of Czechoslovak Children in 1961 to 1963, is also a part of the area of the Burgrave's House. It was built as the eastern gate of the Romanesque fortification system. The gateway, which was soon walled-up, has been preserved to the

STATUE OF ST. BARBARA

EASTERN GATE

present on the ground-floor. The upper floor of the tower served as a prison, especially for debtors. Most of the dates, drawings and inscriptions which the prisoners scratched in the stone ashlars date in the 16th century. At present archaeological finds of Prague Castle are kept in the Black Tower.

The eastern gate and the area in front of it. Adjoining the Black Tower is the eastern gate of Prague Castle.

A Gothic gate for pedestrians has been preserved in the former parkan wall. It originated in earlier building phases. However, the gate proper is Renaissance, having been built in the Sixties of the 16th century. It leads to Opyš, where there is now an observation point on the site of a fortified barbican of the late 15th century from where a fine view of Prague can be obtained. In the 19th century a cannon-shot announcing the precise time was always fired from here at noon.

Built-in in the enclosing wall of the villa at Opyš is a pedestal with a statue of St. Barbara. It is a modern reconstruction of a heavily damaged and unsuitably supplemented Baroque sculpture.

The gate in the wall between the Old Castle Steps and the street called Na Opyši leads to the historic area of the St. Wenceslas Vineyards and to the Neo-Classical Richter Villa overlooking the road Chotkova silnice.

HOUSES IN THE STREET U DALIBORKY

Behind St. George's Convent it is possible to turn off from Jiřská Street to the Golden Lane. Here the way widens into a kind of small square surrounded by several houses, most of which are of Renaissance origin. Some of them form a row linking up with the convent (Nos. 32, 31 and 30), while the others stand in a separate block by Jiřská Street (Nos. 8, 9 and 10).

In the Middle Ages the plots of all these houses belonged to St. George's Convent. According to an analysis of written sources a small Romanesque church consecrated to St. John the Baptist (it supposedly ceased to exist after the mid-16th century) stood on the site now occupied by the group of houses by Jiřská Street. In the late 15th century, when the convent sold the plots of land, new houses began to spring up here. After the fire of 1541 bigger Renaissance houses were built here by a number of persons bound by service to the court. They were also referred to according to their owners' profession: for example, the wheelwright's house, the

painter's house, the controller's house, etc.

Houses No. 8, 9 and 10. House No. 8, called At St. Florian's (U svatého Floriána) was evidently built in 1561 by Jakub Nostran, a servant responsible for Archduke Ferdinand Tyrol's silver. It has a simple Baroque façade (with a painted house sign facing Jiřská Street) and Renaissance ceilings in its interior. In 1966 it was converted into flats and an establishment offering refreshments. The neighbouring house No. 9 originated as a separate building as late as 1663, when an Old Town painter by the name of Václav Vodňanský purchased a part of the lot occupied by house No. 10. The façade facing Jiřská Street is narrow and high and it is broken up in typical Late Baroque style. It is dated in 1765. The biggest house is No. 10, called the Podybnikovský House (after one of its owners – Podybnik – in the 17th century). It was built after 1561 for the court wheelwright Jan Milpoch. Its other owners included, for example, Vilém of Rožmberk, Petr Vok of Rožmberk, the imperial servant Jan Papp, the court controller Tomáš Sauner and, in the early 17th century, even the emperor's court painter Hans van Aachen. The façades of the house are covered with engraved lines imitating ashlars, renewed in 1954. After several adaptations its last Renaissance painted ceiling has been preserved in the interior.

Houses Nos. 32, 31 and 30. This group of houses links up directly with the convent. It originated along the Romanesque wall, likewise on plots of land sold by the convent. House No. 32 (called At the Blue Globe – U modré koule – in the 19th century) was built after the mid-16th century by Jiří Schmidhammer, "the gunsmith and locksmith of His Imperial Grace". In 1593 it was purchased by Gabriel Muryan, the court chimney-sweep, but in the 17th century it once again became the property of the convent. The aim of the convent was to buy the nearest houses because "they were built without permission immediately below the very convent windows, so that the smoke from their chimneys

GOLDEN LANE UNDER SNOW

was an annoyance to the whole convent" and also because "in several places feasts are held and beer and wine are tapped and consequently many nuisances, noisy persons and other ill-mannered people loiter about". House No. 32 has a relatively simple, symmetrical Baroque façade with an axial portal and central dormer. The neighbouring building, No. 31, was built in 1562 by Oldřich Hagle, baker to Archduke Ferdinand Tyrol. In 1603 it was purchased by Rudolph II from his servant Petr Röder, the emperor's aim being to exchange it with the St. Vitus chapter for a part of Vikárka. The house has a Baroque façade with an entrance projection. The house called At the Stone Table (U kamenného stolu), No. 30, was built after the mid-16th century by Markus Rumpolt, Archduke Ferdinand Tyrol's personal chef. After some younger modifications the façades of the house are somewhat heteregeneous: the southern façade has renewed letter graffito, while the others have a simple Baroque appearance dating from the 18th century.

THE GOLDEN LANE, THE WHITE TOWER AND DALIBORKA

The Golden Lane. The picturesque and bizarre little houses in the Golden Lane form an attractive counterpart to the serious and mag-

nificent architecture of the Castle, but at the same time they are the last remainder of the small dwellings which formed an inseparable part of the image of the castle area. The foundation for the origin of the Gold Lane was laid by Vladislav Jagiello when he had the northern parkan wall of the Castle built above the gorge of the River Brusnice. From 1496 the new fortifications in the sector from St. George's Convent to the eastern gate were strengthened by two cannon towers – the White Tower and Daliborka. On its inner side the wall between them was broken up by huge, blind arcades and it was topped by a defence passage. The area of the northern parkan (between the older Romanesque and the new parkan wall) was soon used for the building of modest dwellings. In the 16th century goldsmiths may have lived here, because the older name of the lane was Goldsmiths' Lane. In his report of 1566 the Castle captain mentioned in his report eighteen dwellings in which "many useless families liable to cause fires live at the castle". All the small houses were patently demolished at the time of Rudolph II, when the wall was repaired in 1591. Six years later the emperor granted permission to build twenty-four castle marksmen to build small dwellings in the arches of the parkan wall on condition that they would not open the windows facing Stag Ditch. The marksmen named on the list built their tiny houses in the arches alloted to them. In time, however, their homes fell into the hands of other Castle employees. After the abolition of the institution of the castle marksmen by the Emperor Joseph II the owners of the houses partly took possession also various of the defence passage, using them for the building of annexes. Without permission they made windows and outlets in the wall, which they hewn-out in various ways in order to enlarge the inner space of their homes. In the 19th century most of them had ceased to live here themselves, having leased their houses. During the First Republic care was taken to ensure that the character of the Golden Lane was not spoiled by unsuitable modifications. After World War II the houses were purchased from their owners, four of them being furnished in such a way as to afford an idea of the way of life in various periods. Figurines of alchemists, castle marksmen and servants in life-size execution became parts of the installations. In the Sixties the defence passage and the White Tower were made accessible for a short time. After the abolition of this exposition in the Golden Lane the interiors of the houses gradually began to find use as shops.

The White Tower. On the western side the Golden Lane ends with the widened space in front of the White Tower. This originated as a cannon tower at the end of the 15th century. In the Renaissance period it was rebuilt and in 1585 Rudolph II had prisoners brought here from the Romanesque White Tower, which is now built-in in the central wing between the Second and Third Courtyards. The tower at the end of the Golden Lane also began to be called the White Tower. It is semicircular in shape with an attached right-angled part in the west and a staircase in the east. The ground-floor, which is on a slightly lower level than the ground of the Golden Lane, once served as a torture chamber. It has an irregular dome-shaped vault and is connected with the lower floor, the dungeon, by means of a hole in the floor. The dungeon also has a dome-shaped vault and its originally wider win-

dow recesses were later walled-up apart from small vents. Below the dungeon there is yet another prison in the form of a narrow and wholly dark shaft to which access can be gained only by means of a square hole in the floor. The upper two floors of the White Tower are, on the contrary, adequately illuminated. The rooms have beam ceilings. Numerous inscriptions and drawings have been preserved on the walls and according to the scratched dates most of them fall in the 16th century.

It is known that the head valet Filip Lang, formerly a highly influential courtier, and Kašpar Rudzký, who was guilty of misappropriations from the imperial treasury, were imprisoned in the White Tower during the reign of Rudolph II. Kašpar Rudzký allegedly hung himself on the gold cord from the keys to the treasury. Another well-known prisoner was the English alchemist Edward Kelley. After the Battle of the White Mountain the leaders of the unsuccessful uprising of the Estates and during the Thirty Years' War the imperial officers responsible for military failures were imprisoned in the tower. The white Tower served as a prison until the mid-18th century, later being used for dwelling purposes.

The defence passage. The previously mentioned long defence passage connects up with the White Tower on the level of the first floor. In the direction towards the north it is broken up by loophole windows between which there are embrasures with a rotary wooden drum, designed by B. Ried. In the late 15th century they afforded the marksmen the maximum protection against enemy fire. The present embrasures in the defence passage are modern reconstructions of the original loopsholes.

The tiny houses in the Golden Lane. The projecting part of the individual houses in the Golden Lane are built-on on to the parkan wall below the defence passage. In all they number sixteen and differ in age, width and height. Worthy of special note are the wide house No. 23 in which a staircase leading to the defence passage has been preserved, neighbouring house No. 22, known for the fact that Franz Kafka lived in it (in the years 1916 to 1917) and particularly house No. 20 with a frame upper floor, which represents the best-preserved form of dwelling of the 16th century. The last house, No. 13, on the northern side of the Golden Lane is the only one which has kept to the present the order laying down the way in which the tiny houses were to be built in the arches of the wall: its façade does does not project into the lane at all.

Daliborka. By ascending the staircase in house No. 12 access is gained to the terrace in front of Daliborka. The round cannon tower, set deep into the slope of Stag Ditch, was completed in 1496 as a part of the Jagiello fortifications. This date is hewn in the outer mantle of the tower. A prison was clearly counted with on its lower floors already during the building work and the upper floor was gradually adapted to serve the same purpose. The best-known and simultaneously the first to be imprisoned here was the knight Dalibor of Kozojedy, who afforded protection to the insurgent serfs on the estate of his neighbour. Dalibor was kept in the prison until 1498 and it was after him that it was named. Also imprisoned here, apart from others, were František Tengnagel of Kampa, a courtier of Rudolph II, and František Antonín Špork, a well-known patron of the arts in the 18th century. Daliborka served as a prison until the third quarter of the 18th century.

Nowadays the tower has five floors. It was originally higher and connected with the defence passage, but it was evidently lowered and newly roofed after one of the numerous fires. The entrance floor is reached by means of a staircase. The area of the circular ground-plan is illuminated by four small windows set in deep recesses. Of the ceiling only the beams have been preserved. The upper floor, open to the roof, is of a similar nature. The most interesting part of the tower is the basement, accessible by means of a small passage with a flight of steps in the thickness of the wall. It has a five-part cross vault and in its floor there is a round hole affording access to the dungeon below. In the vault above

the hole it is still possible to see the beam by means of which prisoners were lowered into it. Below the dungeon, which has a dome-shaped vault and only a small ventilation window, there is another prison, again accessible only through a hole in the floor.

VIKÁŘSKÁ STREET

By walking along Vikářská Street we can pass round the cathedral on the northern side. It could have originated as late as after the demolition of the so-called Monastery Church of Prague, which was the seat of the St. Vitus chapter, adjoining Romanesque St. Vitus's Basilica in the north. This building really had a monastery-like appearance from the architectural aspect. Its preserved and archeologically unearthed parts date in the 12th or 13th century. The last, partial reconstruction of the cloister was realized about 1300. After the founding of the Gothic Cathedral of St. Vitus the chapter house was gradually demolished and separate house sprang up here already in the late 14th century. At first all of them belonged to the St. Vitus chapter, but with the passing of time it lost certain houses and plots of land. However, it is difficult to precisely determine houses of the 15th and 16th centuries mentioned in written records.

Mladota's House. The most outstanding building in Vikářská Street is the Chapter Deanery or Mladota's House (No. 37). Its site was originally occupied by at least two houses and still today the building has two architecturally different parts. The palace building of the deanery and school dates in 1591 and it gained its present appearance as the result of the reconstruction carried out by the dean Adam Ignác Mladota of Solopysky in 1705. It has an Early Baroque façade which although flat is conspicuously articulated. The coat-of-arms of the builder can be seen in its triangular tympanum. Preserved in the eastern part of the ground-floor is the room of the former chapter library with an interesting vault, which was decorated with wall paintings in the years 1724 to 1726. The painter concerned, Jan Vodňanský, created ideal portraits showing

LOWER STAG DITCH

a number of eminent personages – the canons of the St. Vitus chapter (among them, for example, the chronicler Kosmas, Beneš Krabice of Weitmile and Václav Hájek of Libočany). The neighbouring part, formed by lower wings round a small courtyard, has a much simpler appearance. The house on this site is documented as belonging to the "supreme baumeistr" B. Ried till 1518.

Mihulka. From the courtyard a passage leads to the open part of the northern parkan with the tower called Mihulka. This name dates from the 19th century and it is evident that the tower was not previously named and was successively called (according to written reports) the New Tower, the Round Bastion, the Laboratorium or the Swedish Laboratorium and the Powder Tower. B. Ried built it as a part of the northern parkan wall in the late 15th century. It was the biggest of the cannon towers intended to defend the Castle against possible attack and siege from the northern side. It was remarkably well-provided for the fulfilment of its function. Its lowest floor, dug deep below the level of the parkan, has a massive stone vault and small loopholes for light fire arms. On the ground-floor and the first floor there are cupola-shaped vaults and bigger loopholes for cannons.

They have ventilation holes and sliding wooden covers. The top floor has a flat ceiling and below the roof, covered with shingle until 1932, its appearance of the late 16th century, when the tower was terminated with an open area with a parapet round its periphery, has been preserved.

Although Mihulka was well-equipped, its defence qualities were never tested in practice. In 1569 the well-known cannon-caster and bell-founder Tomáš Jaroš lived in it, at Rudolph II's time alchemists worked in it and in the 17th century it was used for the storage of gunpowder. In 1645 the building scribe drew attention to the danger of an explosion – and four years later such an event really occurred through the fault of the Swedish garrison. Thanks only to the fact that the tower was well-built it survived the catastrophe, although it suffered heavy damage. In 1754 it fell to the St. Vitus chapter and was very inadequately maintained. The apartments of the sacristans were still situated here in 1950. After its reconstruction, completed in 1980, an exposition of Rudolphian culture and art was installed in Mihulka.

Other houses. The following houses Nos. 38 and 39 and a part of No. 40 have a uniform façade of very little architectural interest. After 1559 the master mason Oldřich de Savosa (later the imperial architect Ulrico Avostalis) built a house here and the house of the "distillers", later, from the end of the 17th century, called the imperial "light chamber", stood here. At the time when the imperial court resided in Prague the "valet over light" lived here. Documented as existing in the 16th and 17th centuries is the gunsmiths' house in which cannon-casters lived. It was connected with the neighbouring Foundry. In 1620 the apartment of a cannon-caster, later of the "old royal clockmaker" Jost Bürgi and the butler Claudius, was situated here. Finally, this site was occupied by the old chapter school, built after the Hussite wars by Zikmund, and the house of the building administration of the church, perhaps also with the house of the stonemasons.

Vikárka. The most important building was, however, the Old Vicarage, which gave its name to the whole street. This building was of Romanesque origin (a part of its foundations was discovered during research in house No. 40 and a part in the imperial stable below the Rudolph Gallery). The known fact that Rudolph II exchanged a part of the Old Vicarage with the chapter in order to be able to demolish it in the course of the construction of the northern palace wing corresponds to this. Another exchange came about in 1754, when Maria Theresa needed certain chapter houses for the western part of the just founded Institute of Gentlewomen. In place of these the chapter gained most of the houses in Vikářská Street, the Foundry and Mihulka. The chapter vicars were accommodated in No. 38 (the so-called Small Vicarage) and No. 39 (the Big Vicarage). Below a part of the long, raised ramp, from which the present entrances to Vikárka leads, is the huge masonry of the foundations of the northern steeple of St. Vitus's Cathedral, whose construction was started during the reign of Vladislav Jagiello. From the one room of the "beer taproom" on the ground-floor of the Big Vicarage an inn gradually developed during the first six months of the 19th century. The writer Svatopluk Čech set the plot of his tale The Excusion of Mr. Brouček to the

15th Century in this environment. In the years 1964 to 1965 house No. 39 along with a part of No. 40 was rebuilt for the Vikárka Restaurant, which since 1990 has also used the reconstructed interior of the former Foundry.

The Foundry. The Foundry building could not originate until the Renaissance period, when it was by then possible to build by the parkan wall, which until then had had to remain unsurrounded by buildings for defence reasons. The Foundry – even if only in a provisionary form – evidently already existed after the fire of 1541, when it was necessary to replace a large number of destroyed cannons and bells. Reports from 1569 refer to the bad state and impossibility of use of the Foundry. In 1571 the emperor allotted financial means for the building of a new one. The casting of a large number of cannons was recorded during the Thirty Years' War (1632, 1645). In 1723 two stables were established in the Foundry. After a short period, during which the Foundry belonged to the St. Vitus chapter, it was sold back to the court administration, which needed space for other stables before

GATE TO THE SOUTHERN WING

VIEW FROM THE POWDER BRIDGE

PACASSI GATE

the coronation of Leopold II in 1791. The <u>building still served for the stabling of horses in 1918.</u>

POWDER BRIDGE AND THE EMBANKMENT

The northern gate and the embankment. A passageway in the northern wing (below the Spanish Hall) affords access to the Powder Bridge. While the <u>remainders of the Renaissance gate</u> of huge, roughly worked ashlars <u>are inside the passageway, the gate proper in the</u> <u>northern façade is a work of the Theresian reconstruction. It is also called the Pacassi Gate after its designer.</u> It leads to a huge embankment which in 1770 replaced a bridge of 1534. The stone pillars are still concealed in the embankment, but their upper parts were

EXHIBITION IN THE RIDING-SCHOOL

TERRACE OF THE RIDING-SCHOOL

insensitively demolished during the construction of the collector below the road to the Castle in 1987. The individual pillars and masonry of the area in front of the gate are at least indicated by a different colour of the paving.

The Riding-school. The street U Prašného mostu continues beyond Stag Ditch and its western front is mainly formed by the façade of the Riding-school, built in the late 17th century (J. B. Mathey).

The short entrance façade of the Riding-school is decorated with stucco reliefs of jumping horses, weapons, busts of Turks and rich scrolls. In 1918 the relief of the imperial eagle was removed from its place above the entrance. The façade is adjoined by a short side wing and an additionally built narnarrow gallery which faces the street with blind windows only. The real windows, which are much bigger, look out on a terrace, laid out in the manner of a garden, on the roofs of garages built in 1952 on a site originally occupied by a summer riding-school. Although the idea of converting the Riding-school into an exhibition hall was of earlier origin, it was realized after a project by the architect P. Janák as late as the years 1948 to 1949.

The Riding-school Court. Linking up with the façade of the Riding-school in northerly direction is an enclosing wall with three Renaissance gates which lead to the Riding-school Court. However, the gate by the Riding-school is a modern copy, the original having been demolished during the construction of the collector.

From the late 16th century the present area was occupied by a carpenters' yard founded on the site of vineyards. New stables and residential and out-buildings were gradually built here, some of them having been preserved in a reconstructed form to the present: in particular the house of the master of the hounds (now the seat of the Fire Brigade) and, opposite the Riding-school, a stable with a forge (now workshops and storerooms).

The Pheasantry and Lumbe's Garden. Lying further to the west is the territory of the former Pheasantry, founded by Rudolph II in 1604. A pond of the 16th century, to which water was conducted by wooden piping from the pond system at Litovice, has been preserved here. Apart from rare species of pheasants, documents exist in respect of the breeding of eagles here. The Pheasantry was used as a camp by occupying armies (the Swedes in 1649 and the French in 1741), which always caused great damage here.

In the years 1971 to 1977 a large burial-ground of the 9th and 10th centuries was subjected to archeological research on the territory of the Pheasantry. Some graves even contained gold and silver jewellery documenting the intensive contacts which the Přemyslids had with the Great Moravian Empire. Jewels imported from Moravia and others produced in Bohemia after Great Moravian models were also found. A part of the burial-ground was excavated under very difficult conditions already in 1952 in the course of the construction of garages to the south of the Riding-school. The last preserved graves were discovered in the narrow wing of the gallery of the Riding-school in the years 1984 to 1985.

The green zone to the north of Stag Ditch continues further to the west with the so-called Lumbe's Gardens. K. Lumbe, a surgeon, joined these plots of land to form a continuous garden in the mid-19th century. It is now used by the horticultural department of Prague Castle. Preparations are currently being made for the new laying-out of this area.

The Stable Court. In the direction away from Stag Ditch the opposite front of the street U Prašného mostu is formed by an enclosing wall with gateways and buildings belonging to the Stable Court. Situated here are the house of the foremen of the masons (formerly the dwelling of the administrator of the Ball-games) Hall, the house of the gardeners and a Renaissance house. This was connected by means of a secret imperial passage on the upper deck of the bridge with the part of the passage leading to the Royal Garden. The still preserved part of this communication passes between the

HOUSES SURROUNDING STABLE COURT

house of the gardener and the former small ball-games hall, which in 1680 was converted into a theatre, in the late 18th century into a stable and during World War II into a garage. In 1792 state stud horses were kept in the stables surrounding the court, where the soldiers who looked after them were also accommodated. At that time the whole area was called The Court of Stallions.

The Lion Court. The end of the front on the eastern side of the street U Prašného mostu is formed by the Lion Court of 1581, built to replace an older wooden menagerie. The building is still Renaissance in its core, but it has undergone several reconstructions, especially since the breeding of beasts of prey was stopped before the mid-18th century. The Lion Court was converted into the restaurant of the present in the years 1967 to 1972.

LION COURT

ENTRANCE TO THE ROYAL GARDEN

THE GARDENS OF PRAGUE CASTLE
THE ROYAL GARDEN

The Royal Garden was founded by Ferdinand I in 1534 to the north of the Castle, on the site of older vineyards, which he gradually purchased from their owners, beyond the gorge of the River Brusnice.

After the unsuccessful beginning of the sovereign the garden gradually acquired a noble Renaissance appearance, finally gaining renown for its botanical rarities and exotic plants from remote countries. The first tulips in Central Europe blossomed in the Royal Garden in the Sixties of the 16th century, later spreading from here to Holland. The garden

BALUSTRADE WITH STATUES

was a centre of great interest also during the reigns of Maxmilián II and Rudolph II. From the very beginning the rulers enriched it with a number of buildings serving for the entertainment of the court society. After the unfavourable period of the Thirty Years' War the garden enjoyed a new era of flourish in the last quarter of the 17th century. It was Barocized by a gardener by the name of Zinner in cooperation with M. B. Braun and K. I. Dienzenhofer in the Thirties and Forties of the 18th century. Great damage was also caused here by the war events which marked the beginning of the reign of Maria Theresa. In the late 18th and particularly in the early 19th century the ornamental flower-beds were abolished and the garden began to be changed into an English park in accordance with then contemporary taste. This natural form with traces of the Renaissance and Baroque conceptions has been preserved to the present.

The garden has never been permanently accessible to the public, possibilities of visiting it always being exceptional. Not until March 1990 was the Royal Garden made accessible throughout the summer season of every year.

The main entrance to the Royal Gardens leads from the west, from the street U Prašného mostu. It originated here in 1742 on the site of the former Poultry Court. The path

CENTRAL PART OF THE FORMER BAROQUE GREENHOUSE

behind the grille-type gate with gilded details begins by the Lion Court and the Renaissance houses by the Stable Court with a short avenue of shaped horse chestnut trees. The entrance part of the garden is closed by a terrace with a balustrade with sculptures of playing children and lions. This group of statues from M. B. Braun's workshop, dating about 1730, now partly consists of copies. On a lower elevation below the terrace there is a circular fountain behind which there are tall trees, especially beeches. Standing on the left of the terrace, by the enclosing wall, is an Empire greenhouse of 1820, the presidential villa being situated on the right. Its centre is formed by the preserved part of a destroyed Baroque greenhouse built by K. I. Dienzenhofer in 1731, the side wings having been added in the years 1947 to 1949.

At about the one third mark the garden is divided by the so-called Central Place, lined with a low parapet and tall lime and horse chestnut trees. This area was once a playground between the gate from the street Mariánské hradby and the façade of the Big Ball-games Hall. Its outstanding feature is a fountain with a statue portraying Hercules battling with a dragon, the work of J. J. Bendl of 1670.

The Big Ball-games Hall was built by B. Wolmut from 1567 to 1569 on the southern boundary of the Royal Garden, immediately above the slope of Stag Ditch. At that time it was the third building intended for ball games at Prague Castle. In the Baroque period the Big Ball-games Hall was converted into a riding-school and stable and during the reign of Joseph II it became a military storehouse. In the Twenties it developed static problems and on the eve of the end of World War II it was hit

GROUP OF STATUES NIGHT

ROYAL GARDEN

CENTRAL SQUARE WITH THE HERCULES FOUNTAIN

FROM THE PRESIDENTIAL VILLA

by artillery fire and destroyed to such an extent that practically only its peripheral walls remained. Its reconstruction, completed in 1952, was headed by the architect P. Janák.

The building of the Big-games Hall is a characteristic manifestation of Renaissance architecture influenced by Italian and mediated by Antique models. However, this applies only in the case of its most complicated northern façade. Its other façades are much simpler, this corresponding to their orientation and importance. The northern front is divided up by huge sandstone half-columns whose capitals bear heavy architraves. The fields between them are broken up by big arches, the end fields indicating a non-existing division into two

RENAISSANCE AND MODERN GRAFFITO ON THE BALL-GAMES HALL ▶

NORTHERN FAÇADE OF THE BALL-GAMES HALL

floors. The stone elements were covered with a coating and painted elements, which are still visible in places. The wall with arches is covered with rich graffito decoration, which has had to be restored several times. Along the sides of the arches below the cornice always two allegorical figures symbolize the elements, the virtues and free art. In the early Fifties the unpreserved part of this decoration in the centre was replaced with formally identical figures which, however, differ as regards contents. They clearly represent allegories of industry (with the symbol of the Five-year Plans) and agriculture.

In front of the façade there is a group of statues Night by M. B. Braun of 1734. Its counterpart Day was destroyed by Prussian bombardment in 1757.

During its last reconstruction the interior of the Ball-games Hall was divided into a central hall and two vestibules. The reinforced concrete vault is a copy of the unpreserved Renaissance vault. For a number of years during which the Ball-games Hall was inacessible to the public large tapestries from the Anthony and Cleopatra cycle hung on its walls. The building now serves mainly for the organization of short-term exhibitions, concerts and solemn assemblies.

The Ball-games Hall was joined in the west by a long and narrow shooting-ground which in the Baroque period was converted into stables. In the east

the sunny edge of Stag Ditch was reserved for an orangery which served for the cultivation of citrus fruits at the time of Rudolph II. In the Fifties of the present century a part of the former orangery was converted into a greenhouse. Among the well-grown trees from the "Central Place" towards the east we can find, for example, the tulip tree and the gingko, several Turkish hazels and the torso of a big false acacia.

A giardinetto, a regular composition of flower-beds, characterizes the eastern-most part of the Royal Garden. The bronze Singing Fountain in the centre is the work of T. Jaroš of the years 1564 to 1568, the model for it having been created by F. Terzio. Water flows to the top from the figure of a bag-piper (the only part of the original fountain replaced with a copy) and falls on the upper bowl supported by figures. From here it falls on to the much wider lower bowl which gives out a ringing sound under the drops of water. This "song of the fountain" can best be heard directly below it.

The noble architecture of the Royal Summer Palace, also justifiably called Queen Anne's Summer Palace, is an object of admiration at the very eastern end of the garden. Sometimes it is incorrectly called Belvedere. Ferdinand I had it built in 1538 after a model created by Paolo della Stella. By 1550 the ground-floor had been completed along with the arcaded gallery and its rich relief decoration, on which Italian stonemasons

GIARDINETTO IN FRONT OF THE ROYAL SUMMER PALACE
ROYAL SUMMER PALACE AND THE SINGING FOUNTAIN

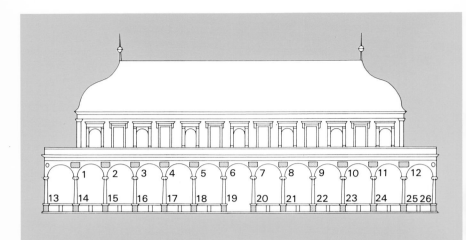

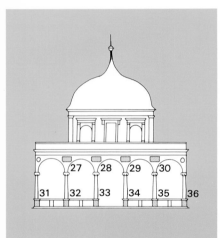

Northern side:
27 Battle between a horseman and a footsoldier
28 Perseus liberating Andromedes
29 Perseus and Phineus
30 Pegasus
31 Hercules and Cerberos
32 Captured commander
33 Welcome in front of the gate
34 Mucius Scaevola putting his hand in the fire
35 Curtius's leap into the abyss
36 Hercules battling with a lion

THE ROYAL SUMMER PALACE – RELIEFS

Western side:
1 Jason fighting with a dragon
   for the Golden Fleece
2 Ferdinand I and Anna Jagiello
3 Wild boar hunt
4 Venus in Vulcan's workshop
5 Man reaping corn
6 Vulcan and Mercury
7 Jupiter and Ganymedes
8 Venus with Amor
9 Danae
10 Leda with swan
11 Abduction of Europe
12 Kadmos fighting with a dragon

13 Hercules with columns
14 Alexander cutting the Gordian knot
15 Alexander and his wife Darei
16 Alexander and Diogenes
17 Men carrying spoils
18 Priestess during sacrifice
19 Flight from Troy
20 Captive
21 Man with keys
22 Female wolf of the Capitol
23 Intoxicated Silenus
24 Apollo and Marsyas
25 Seated ephebe
26 Hercules and Kakus

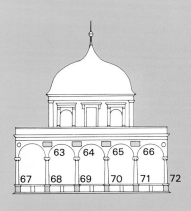

Southern side:
63 Boar hunt
64 Atalanta on a hunt
65 Meleagros conquering a boar
66 Man carrying boar's head
67 Hercules with hind
68 Scene from Bacchanic procession
69 Scene from Bacchanic procession
70 Centaur Nessus carrying off Deianeir
71 Satyr carrying a hind
72 Hercules and the Cretic bull

Eastern side:
37 Ferdinand I out hunting
38 Man with donkey
39 Man with lion
40 Taking away of captives
41 Man with camel
42 Battle scene
43 Battle against Muslims
44 Battle of horsemen
45 Battle scene
46 Charles V freeing captives
47 Battle scene
48 Charles V on horseback
49 War trophies

50 Bust of Silenus
51 Bacchus and satyr
52 Female satyr with child
53 Satyr carrying a wild boar
54 Female satyr with child
55 Satyr playing bagpipes
56 Female satyr feeding child
57 Satyrs with grapes
58 Satyr with stag
59 Hunter with dog and trophy
60 Hunters with trophies
61 Lion hunt
62 War trophies

FERDINAND I AND ANNA JAGIELLO – RELIEF ON ROYAL SUMMER PALACE

DETAIL OF THE SINGING FOUNTAIN

ARCADED GALLERY ROYAL SUMMER PALACE

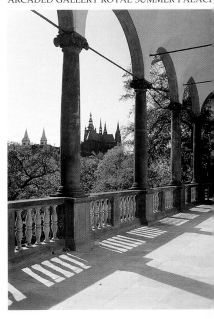

worked. The superstructure of the first floor is the work of H. Tirol and B. Wolmut of after 1552. Under Wolmut's supervision another floor was built up to 1560. It was provided with a unique roof truss covered with copper plate. The roof was decorated with red and white stripes and the

painted emblems of the Czech Kingdom. The decision of Joseph II of 1779 to have this noble building, intended for the entertainment of the court, placed at the disposal of the army was a tragedy for the Summer Palace. When the artillery laboratory established here was successfully removed after the exertion of great efforts the building was renewed and reconstructed in 1836. In the course of this work P. Nobile built a monumental staircase here. From 1928 to 1930 the Summer Palace was repaired under the supervision of J. Plečnik and from 1952 to 1955 it was reconstructed by P. Janák and B. Hacar. On that occasion particularly the damaged vaults of the arcaded gallery were secured. The sculptural decoration was again restored. The last reconstruction of the Royal Summer Palace to date was realized from 1988 to 1991. However, during the work involved a fire broke out in 1989 which caused serious damage to a part of the Renaissance roof truss and its covering.

The one-storeyed core of the building is surrounded by a light arcaded gallery with a terrace on the first-floor level. The arcades are decorated with numerous figural reliefs with themes inspired by Classical mythology, history and the time of the building – before the mid-16th century. The symbolic dedication of the Summer Palace to Queen Anne is expressed by one of the reliefs on the western façade. A rich frieze with a sculptured acanthus and leaf decoration runs below the cornice with a carved balustrade with the motif of the order of the Golden Fleece. The corners of the arcades are decorated with the Czech, Hungarian and Austrian emblems. Apart from a staircase of the first half of the 19th century, the ground-floor features two halls with preserved Renaissance vaults. On the first floor there is one big hall with a wooden coffered ceiling built in the manner of a barrel vault. The walls are decorated with pillasters and wall paintings, all dating from the reconstruction carried out in the 19th century. The themes of the individual scenes from Czech history were approved by the Emperor Franz Joseph I himself and the cartoons for them were made by Ch. Ruben.

The Summer Palace now serves mainly for exhibitions of creative art and artistic crafts, but its pure Italian architecture is itself the main exhibit.

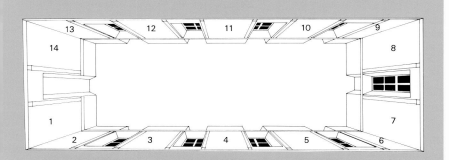

WALL PAINTINGS ON THE FIRST FLOOR OF THE ROYAL SUMMER PALACE

1 Baptism of Prince Bořivoj
2 Death of St. Wenceslas (936 ?)
3 Břetislav I bringing the relics of St. Adalbert (1039) from Poland
4 Coronation of Vratislav II as Czech king (1185)
5 Přemysl Otakar I and Vladislav after their conciliation
6 Václav I on his way to a tournament
7 Přemysl Otakar II's expedition against the pagan Prussians (1254)
8 Charles IV founding a university in Prague (1348)
9 Battle of Lipany (1434)
10 Coronation of Albrecht Hapsburg as Czech king (1438)
11 Rudolph II in front of the torso of a Classical statue
12 Defence of Prague against the Swedes (1648)
13 Joseph II distributing alms on the occasion of hunger in Prague (1772)
14 Leopold II at the Royal Society of Sciences

TERRACE ABOVE THE NEW CASTLE STEPS

THE SOUTHERN GARDENS

The southern gardens originated gradually on the site of the fortifications below Prague Castle. The original slope in front of the Romanesque wall was considerably uneven. From the south a path of access led to the southern gate, which was later abolished and walled-up in the building of the Old Royal Palace. During the reign of Charles IV a parkan wall and a ditch were built and during the Late Gothic period this system was perfected with cannon bastions. Only when the fortifications lost their importance could the area be used for other purposes. In 1559 the governor Ferdinand Tyrol had a private garden laid out in the westernmost part of the ditch, which he had filled in. His garden was connected with the New Building which he had erected and which later became a part of the southern wing. A summer palace, the so-called Bugler's Tower, originated in the garden only to be demolished in the 18th century. Apart from this structure, an aviary and Rudolph II's private bath were also built. From the first half of the 18th century this part began to be called the Garden of Paradise (Rajská zahrada). It was not until the 18th century that small gardens began to originate on other sites of the fortification system. During the Theresian reconstruction the ground in front of the southern façade was levelled with huge banks and a new avenue connected the Garden of Paradise with the area in front of the eastern gate. After the storms of 1848, when the Castle again began to be viewed from the military aspect, a new southern wall with battlements and loopholes was built, but the area was changed into a natural English park already in the latter half of the 19th century. During the period of the First Republic the desolate southern gardens were newly laid out after a project of the architect Josip Plečnik. It was the first of many tasks with which he was entrusted at Prague Castle. In 1960 the Hartig Garden with a Music Pavilion was connected with the southern gardens. In the Sixties and Seventies the southern gardens were regularly accessible during promenade concerts held on Saturdays and Sundays, but from 1985 they were closed for a long time due to the renewal of the underground network. The extensive damage caused to the southern gardens during this period necessitated their

ENTRANCE TO THE GARDEN

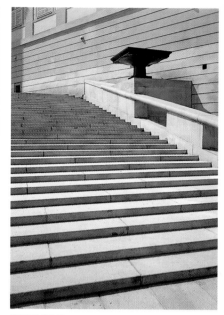

STEPS IN THE GARDEN OF PARADISE

reconstruction. The first part of the gardens (the Garden of Paradise and a part of the Garden on the Ramparts up to the Ludvík Wing) was opened to the public in 1991 and the remaining part of the Garden on the Ramparts two years later.

Three entrances lead to the southern gardens: from the west from Hrad-

čanské Square, from the east from the Opyš observation point and in the middle from the Third Courtyard by means of J. Plečnik's so-called Bulls' Staircase. However, the first of them is considered to be the main entrance. Above the New Castle Steps a small landing with a balustrade adjoins the masonry of the southern promontory.

GRANITE BOWL

MATTHIAS PAVILION

LUDVÍK WING AND OPEN-AIR THEATRE

Here the brick wall with battlements is broken up by a double portal with a pseudo-Classical half-column in the centre. It originated after a design by J. Plečnik.

THE GARDEN OF PARADISE

Immediately beyond the entrance the visitor finds himself on a projection with a decorative sandstone amphora in a niche of the southern façade. This landing is the beginning and the narrowest part of the enormous staircase which takes up a considerable part of the Garden of Paradise. Originally the raising of a monolith with a capital which was supposed to form a kind of lantern for an ever-burning light and at the same time a plinth for a sculpture of the Czech lion with the double Slovak cross was counted with here. A narrow staircase branch directly by the southern façade of the Castle leads to the space below the staircase and to the so-called Wine Cellars below the southern wing. The entrance is emphasized by a square bowl of black stone and a small fountain with a bronze gargoyle.

The lower elevation of the Garden of Paradise is formed by one undivided grassy area demarcated by a granite edge stone.

Standing in its centre is a round bowl hewn from a single block of Mrákotín granite. On the path running along the southern façade J. Plečnik left an older Japan pagoda tree and on the opposite side a centuries' old yew tree, the oldest tree in the Castle gardens.

In 1617 the Matthias Pavilion was completed in the sharp corner of the wall, which attains a considerable height above the New Castle Steps. This small round building with a pointed copper roof is decorated

CRETACEOUS MARLY
LIMESTONE PYRAMID
AT THE OBSERVATION POINT ▶

inside with a painted ceiling with the emblems of the countries of Matthias's empire (of the 17th century) and a decorative painting by J. Navrátil on the walls (of the 19th century). The area surrounding the pavilion was laid out after a part of Plečnik's designs. Standing on a small wall is a bronze statue The Good Shepherd by J. Kalvoda of 1922.

The <u>boundary between the Garden of Paradise and the Garden on the</u>

HARTIG'S GARDEN

MUSIC PAVILION

<u>Ramparts</u> was demarcated by Baroque fencing, but now it is <u>marked by a row</u> of newly planted <u>hornbeams.</u> Only the edge pillars have been preserved of the original fencing.

VIEW FROM THE BULLS' STAIRCASE
MOUTH OF THE BULLS' STAIRCASE

THE GARDEN ON THE RAMPARTS

The <u>narrow band of the Garden on the Ramparts begins with a Baroque fountain</u> of 1703. It was transferred here from the Garden of Paradise and placed in the centre of a regularly divided flower-bed. Running through the garden from here to Opyš is a <u>straight observation path</u> with big lawns and well-grown trees. The botanical specialities in the western half of the Garden on the Ramparts include in particular the Japan pagoda tree, the Chinese metasequoia, the paulonnia and the common catalpa.

<u>The beautiful view of Prague inspired the architect J. Plečnik</u> to lower the defence wall and newly modify its crown. He enriched the garden with

DETAIL OF THE DECORATION

columns terminate with capitals of white marble and parapet panels of the same material are set between them. Further on J. Plečnik placed a big semicircular observation structure with a slender pyramid. However, this has not been preserved in its original form, since it was rebuilt in the Sixties. Linking up with this observation structure lower down in the slope is the smaller area of the Hartig Garden with the round Music Pavilion of the Twenties of the 18th century. Its ground-floor opens on to the garden and inside it has stucco and painted decoration. The Hartig Garden is decorated with six sandstone sculptures by M. B. Braun. These are not, however, historically connected with Prague Castle. They were transferred to their present site from the château at Štířin near Prague.

Opposite the semicircular observation structure the façade of the southern wing is broken up by the so-called Bulls' Staircase whose details again betray the fact that the architect J. Plečnik was frequently and happily inspired by Classical architecture. In the centre of the garden there is now an open-air theatre in front of the mouth of the staircase. It was completed in 1991.

Below the Ludvík Wing it is impossible to overlook the two sandstone obelisks marking the places where the imperial governors Jaroslav Bořita of Martinic (at the foot of the façade) and Vilém Slavata of Chlum

several observation structures which are at the same time rare samples of his masterly work. The first of them is an observation pavilion which is called the Small Belvedere. Its granite

GARDEN ON THE RAMPARTS

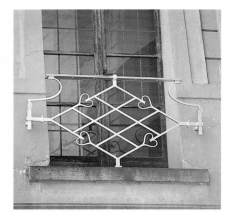

GILDED GRILLE
WITH LIME LEAVES

GRILLE WITH STATE EMBLEM

FOUNTAIN BELOW STAIRCASE

RELIEF DECORATION OF DOOR

SCULPTURE ON THE VOISSURE
OF THE ENTRANCE

BOUNDARY BETWEEN THE
GARDEN OF PARADISE AND
ON THE RAMPARTS

☐ BAROQUE FOUNTAIN

☐ BELLEVUE PAVILION

☐ GATE TO THE VINEYARD
AND ALPINIUM

☐ SLAVATA'S OBELISK
BELOW THE LUDVÍK WING

☐ DECORATED CEILING
OF THE BELLEVUE PAVILION

☐ MONOLITH
OF THE MORAVIAN BASTION

(by the path in the garden) fell during the defenestration in 1618. Vilém Slavata's obelisk also marks the then level of the sloping ground. J. Plečnik provided it with a remarkable balustrade of polished granite.

The semicircular tambour adjoining the façade of the Theresian Wing is a transformer station which unfortunately replaced the much lower aviary which Plečnik built on the foundations of a Late Gothic cannon bastion. Between the transformer station and the Empire gardener's cottage, originally a guard-house, is one of the foundation arches of the Theresian Wing, modified to serve as

SO-CALLED SAMSON'S FOUNTAIN

MORAVIAN BASTION

BEHIND THE GARDEN ON THE BASTION

the entrance to the southern courtyard of the Old Royal Palace. The lower part of the high palace façade dates after 1135 and parts of the solid poygonal fortification elements with which it was strengthened have been preserved.

Further to the east the southern wall is broken up by a small gate used to enter the vineyards and the rock garden on the slope. The bronze head of a woman on the top of the gate is the work of the sculptor D. Pešan, who often created details for Plečnik's buildings or furniture. The original of the sculpture has not been preserved, however. The gate is now decorated with its reconstruction realized in 1990 after older photographic documentation.

J. Plečnik's biggest pavilion is the one called Bellevue on the raised terrace below the Institute of Gentlewomen. The appearance of the enclosing wall is in keeping with its monumental architecture, characterized by columns recalling Ancient Egypt. On the supporting wall below the pavilion J. Plečnik placed the originals of Platzer's putti – torch-bearers, which were replaced with copies in the Third Courtyard. On the area opposite Bellevue he had an Early Baroque sculpture which had formerly stood in the First Courtyard

placed on the fountain after his own design (with the emblem of Slovakia). The fountain is called Samson's Fountain, but this name is incorrect. The hero battling with a lion is Hercules rather than Samson.

The remarkable trees in this part of the garden include an ancient over-hanging beech and a Chinese hazel. Several young Turkish hazel trees, a rare sight in this country, grow along the path in the direction of Opyš.

J. Plečnik's last outstanding building in the Garden on the Ramparts is the Moravian Bastion which projects behind the southern fortification wall below the façade of Lobkowicz Palace. Its peripheral brick wall is broken up by oval windows and a grille-type gate. The wooden pergola is borne by sandstone columns. President T. G. Masaryk and his friends used to sit at the oval granite table. The main feature of the Moravian Bastion is the slender, over eleven metres high granite monolith with an Ionic capital which bears a gilded globe with stylized flashes of lightning. The entrance from the Garden on the Ramparts to the observation place in front of the eastern gate of the Castle is still of a provisionary nature and awaits a definite appearance.

THE GARDEN
ON THE BASTION

The name of this garden recalls the older medieval fortifications on the north-western side of Prague Castle. It was not until the Theresian reconstruction that the ground was definitely levelled here. The area in front of the outer entrance to the Spanish Hall was laid out in a park-like manner as late as 1861.

The garden, modified by the architect J. Plečnik in 1930, is very effective. The difference in height between the Fourth Courtyard and the garden proper is covered by a remarkable circular staircase. The small fountain in its centre was added by Š. Malatinec in 1982, although the original conception of the garden evidently counted with a fountain.

The first geometrically regular part of the garden is formed by yew trees in the middle of round edge stones whose top is covered with white gravel.

The next part is of a less severe and seemingly more natural character.

Visible below the entrance portico of the Spanish Hall is the bared masonry of a medieval tower, covered by a pergola with climbing greenery. The enclosing wall in the direction towards the Archbishop's Palace is broken up by a plastic design creating the effect of ashlars. The restaurant called On the Bastion (Na baště) did not form a part of Plečnik's conception. It was built behind the enclosing wall in 1957 to 1958 and later modified.

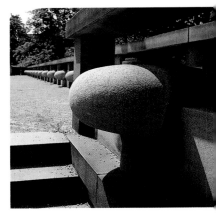

BALUSTRADE IN THE GARDEN ON THE BASTION

From the Garden on the Bastion it is possible to walk along the northern façade of the wing to the Powder Bridge (Prašný most). This connection is made possible by so-called Plečnik's Footbridge, borne by a row of vaulted arches. Its balustrade is supplemented with huge cones of artificial stone. During World War II the air-raid shelter of President E. Hácha of the protectorate was situated below one of the arches of Plečnik's Footbridge.

THE GARDEN ON THE
RIDING SCHOOL TERRACE

The least known and the least frequented of the gardens of Prague Castle which are accessible to the public is the roof garden on the terrace of the Riding-school. Access to it is gained from the street

THE MASARYK OBSERVATION POINT ABOVE UPPER STAG DITCH

U Prašného mostu through a gate next to the Riding-school and via the Riding-school Court, or through a passage way and by means of a staircase in the gallery wing.

Although at first sight the layout of the garden <u>brings Baroque gardens to mind,</u> it is, on the contrary, currently the youngest realization of this type on the area of the Castle. <u>It originated</u> after a design by P. Janák in the Fifties after the building of the garages and repair workshops of the Office of the President of the Republic. In spite of the dense vegetation it is possible to see at least a part of Plečnik's modifications of the northern corner of Stag Ditch with so-called Masaryk's observation

place and vineyards. This terrace is currently awaiting reconstruction.

The used elements were taken from historic gardens. We can see here a high wall of cut hornbeam, regular lawns, low box borders, yews cut in the shape of round loaves, low stone fountains and portable ceramic vases.

The area of the garden on the roof of the garages is lined on two sides by the angle of the building of the Riding-school and the narrow gallery wing. A little known view of the cathedral, a part of the northern fortification wall and the upper part of Stag Ditch can be obtained in southerly direction over a low parapet.

GARDEN ON THE TERRACE OF THE RIDING-SCHOOL

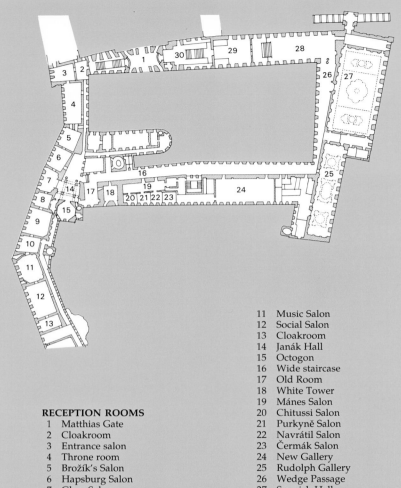

RECEPTION ROOMS

1 Matthias Gate
2 Cloakroom
3 Entrance salon
4 Throne room
5 Brožík's Salon
6 Hapsburg Salon
7 Glass Salon
8 Small Salon
9 Mirror Salon
10 Salon with fireplace
11 Music Salon
12 Social Salon
13 Cloakroom
14 Janák Hall
15 Octogon
16 Wide staircase
17 Old Room
18 White Tower
19 Mánes Salon
20 Chitussi Salon
21 Purkyně Salon
22 Navrátil Salon
23 Čermák Salon
24 New Gallery
25 Rudolph Gallery
26 Wedge Passage
27 Spanish Hall
28 Rothmayer Hall
29 Cloakroom
30 Plečnik's Hall of Columns

CONSOLE WITH ADAM AND EVA BEHIND THE HIGH ALTAR
◄ IN ST. VITUS'S CATHEDRAL

WHAT CANNOT BE VISITED AT PRAGUE CASTLE

There are still many places and buildings on the area of Prague Castle which are not accessible to visitors. Preparations are being made to open up some of them to the public and in other cases access to visitors is counted with. However, some buildings and sites will never be opened up to the public.

At present the representative interiors of the Castle are accessible to the public only exceptionally, as a rule twice a year – in May and October. Only researchers may visit the Castle archives for the purpose of studying archive materials. Other inaccessible interiors such as the rooms of the former apartment of T. G. Masaryk, the crown chamber, the underground areas of archeological excavations and the collection depositories cannot be visited at all. In spite of this – or perhaps just because of it – these places arouse interest which can be at least partly satisfied by more detailed information.

ROOMS USED FOR STATE RECEPTION PURPOSES

The ceremonial reception of eminent visitors to Prague Castle has changed many times in the course of time, but the architecture of the palace has remained unchanged since the last quarter of the 18th century.

Already at the time of its origin the majestic Matthias Gate was the ceremonial entrance to the seat of the sovereign and not the fortification gate. In its interior, on the right, a Rococo staircase with a red stair carpet leads to the first floor. Here there begins a continuous row of reception rooms whose windows face the city and afford a magnificent, ever-changing view. These rooms are usually collectively referred to as the Old Salons, because later new salons originated here. The really old reception rooms were, however, a part of the Old Royal Palace, while the new ones are not older than the Theresian reconstruction of the Castle. Their original appearance has been preserved only exceptionally. Some rooms have even been divided or connected. The decoration of their walls and ceilings has been changed several times and their furniture even more frequently. Their present appearance is thus the result of development: their last reconstruction was realized in the years 1986–1990 and it is quite possible that in a short time their pictorial decoration will be changed and that the description presented here will no longer be precise.

The Cloakroom (by the Matthias Gate). For wholly practical reasons the row of Old Salons begins and ends with a cloakroom. Its decoration and furnishings are relatively simple. It is the only one of the salons to have a plain, undecorated ceiling. Apart from a Baroque cabinet with beautiful and complicated tarsia, attention is attracted chiefly by a large gobelin from the Anthony and Cleopatra cycle, a Brussels work of the 17th century. The individual

CLOAKROOM BY THE MATTHIAS GATE

pieces of this series, the most valuable of the collection of tapestries at Prague Castle, also decorate certain other reception rooms.

The Entrance Salon. It is sometimes called the Children's Salon because of canvasses painted with putti at play. Canvasses cover the whole walls like wallpapers – not here, however, but in the next room which became a part of the Throne Room after the removal of the partition wall. The dominant part of the decoration of the Entrance Salon is again a gobelin of the Anthony and Cleopatra series. Two

ENTRANCE SALON

landscape paintings hang on the blue walls, the work of F. A. Müller of the mid-18th century, as well as two smaller seascapes by an unknown Dutch painter. The stove in the corner is Empire and the furniture Neo-Classical.

The Throne Room. This room originated as the result of the later connecting-up of three original rooms. Three crystal chandeliers, manufactured quite recently at Kamenický Šenov, hang from the ceiling, whose periphery is decorated with stucco ornaments. The walls are covered

with patterned silk wallpaper in a red-and-brown combination. Hanging in the middle of the longest wall (opposite the windows) is a painting portraying the coronation of Ferdinand V, the last crowned Czech king, of 1836. However, it was painted by L. Bucher of Vienna in 1847. The Rococo tiled stove is white and features richly gilded details. Marble-topped tables by the wall harmonize with it. The biggest of the three Persian carpets measures 10 × 5 metres and it is a faithgul copy of the original, which is in London. Most of the welcoming and reception ceremonies take place in this room (and on this carpet).

The Brožík Salon. This salon was named after the outstanding Czech painter Václav Brožík, whose work with themes from Czech history form its decoration. The biggest of the paintings (painted in Paris in 1878) is The Message of King Ladislav to the French Court. It shows the reception of a large delegation of Czech noblemen by the French king Charles VII in 1457. Ladislav Pohrobek asked the king for the hand of the Princess Magdalene, but he died in the same year and the wedding did not take place. The other two paintings by Brožík are much smaller. They are studies for the big historic canvasses with the themes The Election of George of Poděbrady as Czech King and The Founding of Charles University by Charles IV. The brocade wallpaper and the upholstery of the Neo-Classical furniture repeat the same pattern: blue-and-green on the walls and gold on the furniture. The

THRONE ROOM

HAPSBURG SALON

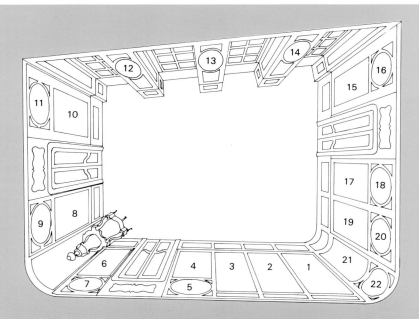

PORTRAITS IN THE HAPSBURG SALON

1. The Emperor
   Franz Stephen of Lotharingia
2. The Empress Maria Theresa
3. The Emperor Joseph II
4. The Emperor Leopold II
5. His consort the Empress Maria Louise
6. The Archduke Ferdinand
7. His consort Maria Beatrix d'Este
8. Marie Amálie, Duchess of Parma
9. Her husband Ferdinand,
   Duke of Parma
10. Archduchess Marie Christina
11. Her husband, Prince Albert
    of Saxony-Cieszyn
12. Archduchess Alzbeta
13. Archduchess Marie Anna
14. Her husband Prince Karel of Lotharingia
15. Archduchess Marie Anna,
    ruler in Lotharingia
16. Archduchess Maria Theresa as a child
17. Queen Marie Antoinette
18. Her consort Louis XVI,
    king of France
19. Archduke Maxmilián, Grand Master
    of the Order of German Knights
20. The Emperor Franz II as a child
21. Queen Marie Karolina
22. Her consort Ferdinand IV,
    king of Naples

richer gilding of the stucco decoration of the ceiling was renewed during the last reconstruction.

The Hapsburg Salon. This salon is the <u>only one</u> to have <u>preserved its original appearance of the late 18th century.</u> Its walls are covered with white panelling with gilded details. <u>Portraits of members of Maria Theresa's</u> family hang on them. The three biggest portraits are of the empress herself, her consort Franz Stephen of Lotharingia (on her right) and her son, her co-ruler and later successor, Joseph II (on her left). Maria Theresa is portrayed as the Czech queen in her coronation garments (preserved to the present), with the St. Wenceslas crown on her head, the sceptre in her right hand and the St. Wenceslas sword at her side. The smaller oblong and oval canvasses portray her children and the seventeen oval portraits above them her daughters-in-law, sons-in-law and grandchildren. The <u>salon has Rococo seating furniture</u> with red upholstery.

The Glass Salon. The bright atmosphere of this room is partly due to the light blue walls and gilded, richly cut chandelier. The gilded ornaments round the periphery of the ceiling are supplemented with motifs of musical instruments, which betray the purpose for which this interior was once used. The <u>Persian carpet</u> of the 20th century <u>is remarkable</u> due to the fact that <u>numerous animal and human figures are portrayed in its rich ornamentation,</u> this being <u>strictly forbidden by Islam.</u> The paintings by anonymous Italian painters depict

GLASS SALON

the Castle of Angels in Rome and a coastal scene with ruins. (Wide glass doors connect the salon with the Janák Hall and other reception rooms in the central and northern wings. More about these further on.)

The Small Salon. The prevailing colour in this room is gold, because apart from the usual gilded chandelier and ornaments on the ceiling, the furniture, the door, the tiled stove and the brocade wallpapers feature the same colour. The <u>painting of St. Paul</u> is the work of the <u>best-known painter of the Czech Baroque, P. J. Brandl.</u> True, we do not know the name of the painter of the other picture, but the change of the name of the work is interesting. Before its restoration in 1983 it was given as The Odd Couple because it portrayed an old man and a young woman. However, after the removal of the overpainting the original portrait of a woman of an age corresponding to that of the man appeared. The figures in the painting

BROŽÍK SALON

MIRROR SALON

are perhaps Philemon and Baucis, known from classical legends.

The Mirror Salon. This room is furnished as a dining-room and (apart from occasions with a large number of participants) some ceremonial lunches and dinners really take place in it. True, the decoration of the wall with mirror panels is not wholly original, but the manner in which they are divided, typical of big reception rooms in the Rococo period, has been preserved. The mirrors were intended to reflect the flames of the candles on the carved and gilded chandeliers and thus improve the illumination of the room. This explains why there are no paintings on the walls. The salon is decorated with gilded ornaments. In one corner there is a decorated tiled stove and in the opposite corner a fireplace of white marble with

a beautiful Rococo clock on the mantlepiece. The large carpet of 1854 comes from south western Persia.

The Salon with a Fireplace. This smaller room got its name thanks to its white marble fireplace. The Neo-Baroque gilded furniture and rich, likewise gilded Rococo chandelier correspond to the gilded textile wallpaper. The tapestry on the front wall is of French origin and evidently formed a part of an 18th-century cycle with a classical theme which has not been preserved.

The Music Salon. This room differs from the others due to its slanting corners. In two of them there are niches with an artificial marble surface. A Rococo tiled stove was situated in one corner and a patinated plaster casting of Braun's group of statues Night from the Royal Garden

SALON WITH FIREPLACE

TILED STOVE IN THE MIRROR SALON

with red upholstery and the stove is Rococo.

The Cloakroom at the Exit. The row of salons in the southern wing ends with a cloakroom whose <u>walls are again decorated with tapestries from the Anthony and Cleopatra cycle.</u> Also to be seen here are two <u>portraits of Spanish noblemen</u> by F. Luycx of the period following the mid-17th century and four <u>engravings</u> by E. Baudet with the <u>theme of the four elements</u> (c. 1700). From the cloakroom it is possible via a passage to reach a decorated balcony or a spacious staircase, which is not of such a ceremonial character of the entrance of honour from the Matthias Gate.

The Janák Hall. <u>After returning to the Glass Salon it is possible to pass</u> through big glass doors <u>to the Janák Hall.</u> It was named after the Castle architect Janák, who modified it in 1937. Its moderately articulated ceiling, plain walls and floor of stone slabs form a contrast to the decorativeness of the Old Salons. Two separate columns of polished granite

JANÁK HALL

DETAIL OF PERSIAN CARPET (GLASS SALON)

(the casting originated in the years 1943 to 1944 in the other. <u>On the opposite slanting corners</u> there are two <u>Brussels gobelins of the 17th century.</u> Their central motif is always a couple of allegorical female figures symbolizing the continents. One gobelin represents Asia and Europe and the other America and Africa. The relatively rich stucco decoration of the ceiling, which has not been preserved in its original form, was renewed according to old photographic documentation in 1988 to 1990.

The Social Salon. The walls of this room are of a simpler nature and there is less gilded ornamentation on the ceiling. The <u>three crystal chandeliers</u> are fairly recent products of the glassworks at Kamenický Šenov. The furniture is Neo-Classical

form the only architectural decoration. Hanging on a wall is a Brussels gobelin from the <u>Months cycle of the 17th century.</u> Two winged female figures symbolize March and April. <u>Another gobelin from the same</u> cycle <u>can be seen in the western part of the hall,</u> which has flat cross vaults on pillars.

The Octogon. From 1644 the <u>court chapel, consecrated to St. Wenceslas</u>

and abolished during the Theresian reconstruction, was situated in this reception salon of the present. Its flat ceiling has ungilded stucco ornaments. <u>Hanging on the walls</u> are <u>three gobelins from the Anthony and Cleopatra cycle.</u> The carved gilded chandelier originated as a copy of the Rococo lighting fixtures in the Old Salons as late as the Eighties of the present century.

RESTORED DECORATION OF THE MUSIC SALON

MUSIC SALON

SOCIAL SALON

The Wide Passage. Several steps lead from the Janák Hall to the Wide Passage. The imperial collections were kept in this connecting wing, built during the reign of Rudolph II. Its present appearance is the result of the modifications of the central wing carried out by the architect J. Fragner in the early Twenties of the 20th century. Connecting up with it on the right is the open interior of the Old Hall with a beam ceiling and Romanesque ashlar masonry. These rooms above the former western gate were closed by a wall (on the right) and the huge White Tower (on the left). The cretaceous marly limestone masonry dates in the period after 1135. The Old Hall is decorated with

two gobelins May – June and August from the Months cycle.

The Romanesque ashlar masonry of the White Tower continues in the walls of the passage. The remainders of brick vaults date in the Rudolphian period. Access to the rooms in the tower is gained by means of a massive iron Empire door and this is why it is sometimes also called the Iron Treasury.

The New Salons. In the central wing the Wide Passage is adjoined by the so-called New Salons, likewise modified by J. Fragner in the Sixties. They are named after the painters whose works decorate them: Mánes, Chitussi, Purkyně, Navrátil and

OLD HALL

ENTRANCE TO THE WHITE TOWER

Čermák. The painted beam ceilings of these rooms date from the time of Ferdinand II, i.e., from about the mid-17th century. They were transferred here from the second floor of this wing, where – in the present offices – they were replaced with flat, reinforced concrete ceilings, in the course of J. Fragner's modifications.

The New Gallery. As a part of the New Salons by the Wide Passage this gallery is a contemporary attempt to create a hall-type interior in the so-called Brussels style. The parquet floors of noble woods and especially the sharp-angled shapes of the huge

lighting fixtures of copper plate are striking features here. However, the resulting impression can hardly be compared with the quality of the historic reception rooms.

The decoration of the Wide Passage. The present decoration of the Wide Passage can only remotely bring the location of the art collections of Rudolph II here to mind. It consists of two gobelins from the Months cycle (September – October and November – December), a Flemish gobelin with the commander Hasdrubal of the early 17th century and a number of paintings with scenes of sea battles painted in the 17th century by

SPANISH HALL (width 21 m, length 43 m, height 12 m)

THE NEW SALONS HAVE PAINTED CEILINGS

M. Platenberg. The last painting in the series is The Abduction of the Sabines by an unknown painter of the 17th century.

The Rudolph Gallery. A flight of steps leads from the Wide Passage to the Rudolph Gallery, which the Emperor Rudolph II built for his collection of paintings. While the room had plain walls at that time in order that there might be maximum space for the hanging of paintings, the walls and the ceiling are now covered with rich relief decoration from the latter half of the 19th century.

The Spanish Hall. In comparison with the neighbouring Rudolph Gallery the Spanish Hall is much bigger, although it is of a similar character. Both interiors were adapted at the same time for the prepared coronation of Franz Joseph as Czech king. However, the Spanish Hall underwent a more complicated process of

ČERMÁK SALON

WIDE PASSAGE

development: it <u>originated in the early 17th century as a double-aisled hall</u> with a number of wooden columns in the centre and with a painted ceiling soffit. Above-lifesize sculptures of fired clay and stucco were situated in niches in the southern wall. The walls were decorated with stucco reliefs, part of which has been preserved to the present. <u>In the first half of the 18th century the hall was raised</u> and the new structure of the roof truss made it possible to remove the columns. The <u>hall was provided with an upper row of windows.</u> During the Theresian reconstruction the niches in the southern wall were walled-up and the painter J. K. Saeckel decorated them with illusive landscape views with ruins. In 1836 these paintings were covered with

COLUMNS IN THE WEDGE PASSAGE

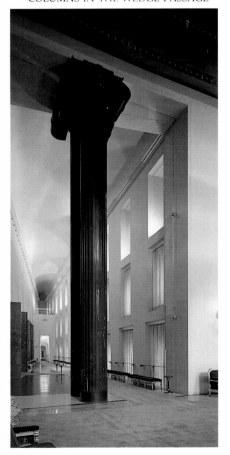

mirrors. The present relief decoration of the hall originated from 1865 to 1968. Contrary to the Rudolphian freely modelled stucco it consists of plaster castings additionally fixed on a wall or the ceiling. The two shorter walls of the hall were designed and built in a wholly new way. They are

ROTHMAYER HALL

decorated with sculptures Art, Science, Trade and Industry by A. la Vigne.

During the day the hall is illuminated by a row of northern windows, artificial illumination being provided by <u>gilded chandeliers and wall lighting fixtures with over two thousand bulbs.</u>

The Wedge Passage. In order to level out the irregular shape of the Second Courtyard N. Pacassi built the so-called Wedge Passage on to the southern side of the Spanish Hall. Its present appearance dates from the Fifties of the present century and it was realized by J. Plečnik's co-worker and successor architect O. Rothmayer. <u>Especially remarkable are the couple of black Ionic columns in the mouth of the passage</u> and details of the hammered balustrades. <u>Gobelins from</u> the Blue Months cycle, produced by a manufactory at La Malgrange in Lotharingia, hang on a wall. Their surface is mainly covered with ornamental decorations, the respective month always being symbolized merely by a relatively small motif in the centre.

The Rothmayer Hall. The Wedge Passage leads to the Rothmayer Hall, a high interior with three rows of windows above each other. A statue of T. G. Masaryk, a work of white Karar marble sculpted by J. Štursa in 1921, stands by the front wall. Originally it was situated in the building of Parliament, after which it was housed for long years in the depository of the National Gallery at Zbraslav. It was placed in its present position in 1991.

The Cloakroom in front of the Spanish Hall. This was completed in 1975 as an accessory of the Spanish Hall, where particularly solemn assemblies of the Central Committee of the Communist Party of Czechoslovakia took place at that time. A granite staircase was built-in in Plečnik's Hall of Columns in the same period. There can definitely be no doubt as to the necessity of a cloakroom and staircase in these places, but their architectural design, especially that of the cloakroom, is, unfortunately, typical of the taste of its time. It is most likely that this part will be rebuilt.

Plečnik's Hall of Columns. J. Plečnik built a high, monumental interior in the neighbourhood of the Matthias Gate by removing all the floors. In front of the windows, which indicate the original manner in which the building was divided up, there are galleries with three rows of granite columns above each other. Simplicity, classical proportions and noble materials – all these enhance the impression created by this interior, which was strongly inspired by Classical architecture.

THE APARTMENT OF T. G. MASARYK

Running from the south-western corner of the Third Courtyard is the semicircular entrance to the so-called tunnel which connects the Third Courtyard with the Second Courtyard. The gate and the whole inner space were designed by the architect Josip Plečnik from 1923 to 1924 as the entrance to the apartment of the president of the Republic. At the most he built an effective spiral staircase leading to the room of the apartment lying at the place of contact of the southern and the central wing on the second floor. Its

PLEČNIK'S HALL OF COLUMNS

walls and vaults are built of unplastered bricks and the shaft of a lift with a round cabin of mahagony and glass passes through it.

At least some of the rooms of the president's apartment have been preserved or recently reconstructed. The passage widens into the effective interior of an Impluvium with a floor of polished granite, a central fountain and ceiling lighting. The walls of the Harp Salon, accessible from the Impluvium, are covered with plate gold and above the portal it is decorated with small, gilded sculptures by D. Pešan. The Social or Green Salon is characterized by wooden columns situated in front of the walls covered

SMALL SPIRAL STAIRCASE

with green drapes. A room on the second floor of the Romanesque White Tower, in which there is a vault with stucco and painted decoration from the time of Rudolph II, has been changed into the Emblem Hall, or the Hall of the First Citizen of the State. Polychromed relief emblems of the countries of the Czech Republic hang on the walls. The table in the centre is made of marble and teak wood and on the pedestal below the top there is the inscription "Obci starosti své osobní podrob" (Subordinate your troubles to those of the community).

TUNNEL
IMPLUVIUM

GOLDEN HARP SALON

DETAIL OF THE DECORATION
OF THE HARP SALON
VAULT OF THE EMBLEM HALL

EMBLEM HALL

On the same floor as the apartment there was a library in which President Masaryk spent a great deal of time. Bookshelves of polished mahogany cover the whole walls and now contain 35,000 books. Masaryk's library was not returned to its original place until 1993. In the Seventies the room was converted into a study for the then president, G. Husák. However, the furnishings of the library were kept in safety in a similar interior on the third floor even if at the cost of the lowering of the shelf walls.

The Lion Fountain on the ground-floor of the southern projection and the Vase Staircase leading to the ground-floor of the southern wing to the Garden on the Ramparts are also connected with the modification of the president's apartment.

THE CROWN CHAMBER

The Crown Chamber, in which the coronation jewels of Czech kings are kept, is without any exaggeration one of the least accessible places at Prague Castle. The only entrance to it is a metal-plated door in the south-western corner of St. Wenceslas's Chapel. In order to open it the seven keepers of the keys have to get together. These persons are: the president of the Republic, the prime minister of the government, the archbishop of Prague, the Chamber of Deputies, the president of the Senate (the president of the Chamber of Deputies acts as his deputy when

VIEW OF THE INTERIOR OF THE OFFICE OF THE PRESIDENT OF THE CZECH REPUBLIC

LION FOUNTAIN

there is no Senate), the Metropolitan Chapter of St. Vitus and the mayor of Prague.

The Crown Chamber has a cross vault with three fields and no coping stones. The ribs of the vault rest on huge sandstone consoles in the form of fantastic human and animal heads. A search for such enormous vault consoles would be in vain in the whole building. The painted decoration of the walls and all the inner furnishings date in 1867. The ornamental painting features, apart from the St. Wenceslas female eagle, a composition of the emblems of Bohemia, Moravia, Silesia, Upper and Lower Lusatia and the Prague and Olomouc archbishoprics.

Standing by the front wall of the chamber is a pedestal on which a cabinet-type receptacle in Neo-Gothic style is placed. On its front side St. Wenceslas is portrayed among angels against a gold background and on the sides can be seen the figures of Vratislav, the first crowned Czech king, and Charles IV, who had the St. Wenceslas crown made. The Latin inscription on the receptable reads: The crown of the Czech kingdom, presented by Charles, margrave of Moravia in the year of our Lord 1345 to St. Wenceslas, here with the other insignia of the kingdom is deposited. 1867

The coronation jewels proper are housed inside the receptacle in leather boxes. They comprise the crown, orb and sceptre. The box containing the crown dates in 1347. Brightly coloured polychromed symbols – the Czech lion and the imperial female eagle – and the date are cut out in its thick leather. The box with the sceptre is of the 19th century and decorated with a small gilded ornament. The orb is deposited in a leather container with the emblem of the Czechoslovak Republic of 1929. (At the time of origin of the crown, however, the orb and sceptre were quite different. Those insignia of the sovereign were used until the 17th century, when they were evidently replaced with the richer ones of the present.) The royal crown was dedicated to St. Wenceslas, the principal provincial saint. At the request of Charles IV this was confirmed by a special document signed by Pope Clement VI, who at the same time established a punishment in the form of ex-communication for any unauthorized person handling the crown. The crown was supposed to be permanently placed on the head of St. Wenceslas and removed only for a coronation or an exceptionally solemn event in Prague or its nearest environs – and for one day only. The crown was in the care of the Metropolitan Chapter attached to St. Vitus's Cathedral, for which service the king paid it 43.2 kilogrammes of silver after a coronation.

The described strict measures were in force to the late 14th century at the most, however. The coronation jewels were then deposited in Karlštejn Castle. After the outbreak of the Hussite wars Zikmund of Luxembourg took them to Hungary, from where they were returned to Karlštejn in 1436. For a short time before the mid-15th century they were also kept at Velhartice Castle and from 1453 to 1619 they were again guarded by two Karlštejn burgraves. During the short period of 1619 to 1620 they were kept in a room of the Land Rolls. Fleeing Fridrich of the Palatinate left them at the Old Town Hall, from where they were returned to St. Wenceslas's Chapel on the same day. During the stormy period of the Thirty Years' War the jewels were alternately kept in a cellar in front of the chapel and in secret places outside Prague, for example, in the cellerage of the parish church at České Budějovice. From the 17th century they were permanently kept in Vienna, returning to Prague only on the occasion of a coronation. In 1791 the jewels were finally taken to Prague Castle, displayed for a whole afternoon for the first time and then placed in safe-keeping along with the crown archives. After a short period during which they were deposited in Vienna in the course of the Prussian-Austrian war they were solemnly returned to Prague in a festively decorated train in 1867, this being their last journey. After being exhibited they were placed in the newly adapted Crown Chamber, where they have remained to the present apart from a short period in 1938 (when they were secretly taken to a safe in a bank in Žilina) and in 1945 (when they were walled-up in the floor of the Old Royal Palace). In the course of the present century the coronation jewels have been exhibited eight times – in 1929, 1945, 1955, 1958, 1968, 1975, 1978 and 1993.

THE CZECH ROYAL CORONATION JEWELS

THE CZECH ROYAL CORONATION JEWELS

The crown, called the St. Wenceslas crown, was most likely made in 1345 of gold plate. It has the form of a coronet consisting of four parts, each of which terminates with a big lily. The individual parts are joined at the top by two curved pieces on which the decorations of an older jewel (coronet or belt) are fastened. At the place where the curved pieces intersect there is a gold cross with a sapphire cameo. In all there are 19 sapphires, 44 spinels, 1 ruby, 30 emeralds and 22 pearls on the crown. The total weight of the crown without the parts made of material is 2,475.3 grammes. It is always exhibited on a special cushion of red velvet with the embroidered Czech emblems of 1867. Some of the stones exceed the lower edge of the crown with the result that if the crown were placed on a hard, level base their beds would be exposed to unnecessary stress.

The sceptre of the first half of the 16th century is 670 millimetres in length, its weight being 1,013 grammes. It is gold and decorated with 4 sapphires, 5 spinels, 66 pearls and hammered and enamel ornaments.

The orb of the first half of the 16th century is also made of gold. It is 220 millimetres in height. On the lower hemisphere there is a hammered relief with scenes from Genesis, while on the upper one there are scenes from the life of King David. In all 8 sapphires, 6 spinels and 31 pearls were used for its decoration.

The coronation mantle, with an ermine stole, belt and maniple of red material with a pattern woven with gold are kept in the depository of historic textile in another place. They originated in the first third of the 17th century as a part of the collection of Czech coronation, royal and electorate textiles, whose other parts are now in Vienna.

As a rule the St. Wenceslas sword and coronation cross are exhibited with the coronation jewels. Both form parts of the St. Vitus treasure.

THE ARCHIVES OF PRAGUE CASTLE

The archives originated in their present form as late as 1920, when the long-standing tradition of storing important state documents and other records in various places in the Castle was kept. Apart from the Crown Archives, the written materials of the Metropolitan Chapter attached to St. Vitus's Cathedral and of the Prague archbishopric as well as the archives of the courts and central institutions which had their seat here (for example, the Czech Chamber, the Court of Appeal, the Land Rolls, the governor's office and the Court Building Office have been kept at the Castle in the course of the centuries. The location of the archives has changed many times and on some occasions they were even removed from the Castle. In the 18th, 19th and early 20th centuries they were partly transferred to Vienna, from where some were returned after 1918. A number of important documents is deposited in the State Central Archives.

The present Archives of Prague Castle concentrate written material and all documentation concerning the Castle, its history and research, building activity, repairs and maintenance. For example, invaluable documents concerning building activity are kept in the funds of the Court Building Office (1540–1860), the Castle Executive office (1860–1918) and the Office of the President of the Republic (1918–1964). The funds of the Union for the Completion of St. Vitus's Cathedral is a source of information not only about the completion work proper, but also about the medieval parts of the cathedral and the finds made in the course of research or during the completion of the cathedral. The Plan Collections, the Old Collection up to 1918 and the New Collection from 1918, contain historic plans of the individual buildings and project documentation pertaining to recently completed reconstructions. Also filed is a number of unrealized projects.

The library of the Metropolitan Chapter of St. Vitus's Cathedral, which contains many rare medieval manuscripts, often beautifully illuminated old prints and music scores, is also in the care of the Archives of Prague Castle. The oldest manuscript on the territory of the Czech state, the Gospel of St. Mark of the 6th century, is also deposited in it.

Documents of historical value also form parts of the Archives of the Metropolitan Chapter attached to St. Vitus's Cathedral.

ARCHEOLOGICAL EXCAVATIONS

Some archeological excavations, covered with a reinforced structure, have remained preserved below the paving of the Third Courtyard. They spread out in front of the entrance to the Old Royal Palace and in the zone along the southern wing. Only a narrow corridor passes through the area of the excavations, leading from the Gothic floor of the Old Royal Palace to the south-western corner of the Third Courtyard. It begins by the foundations of the no longer existing wing of the Old Royal Palace, which was built after the mid-13th century.

The ashlar masonry of the single-naved Church of St. Bartholomew dates in the 12th century. By its apse and at the corner the original level of the ground in the Romanesque period is clearly evident. The original cretaceous marly limestone paving and the foundations of the altar table have been preserved inside the church. A vaulted passage, also of Romanesque origin, connected the church with St. Vitus's Basilica. It was demolished during the reign of Charles IV and the church itself patently ceased to exist as late as the 15th century.

The communication continues through the basement of a bigger house of the 13th century and two Gothic houses. Clearly to be seen on the southern side are the remainders of older stone buildings – the corner of a small house and the masonry of a bigger one with two rooms. These Romanesque buildings date in the late 12th or early 13th century and they are much smaller than the neighbouring Gothic houses.

According to found remainders the oldest dwelling-houses of the 10th and 11th centuries were even more modest. They had the form of simple frame houses with usually one room only. Very often the paths and spaces between the houses were covered with planks and separated by fences made of stakes and wickers. Thanks to the constant dampness of the lower strata of the terrain remainders of wooden structures of this kind have been preserved, for example, below the connecting passage to St. Bartholomew's Church.

The remainders of a defence mound, which protected the castle site from the late 9th century to the first half of the 12th century, are very interesting. A mound-type fortification element had only a limited service life, because it consisted of a heap of earth strengthened inside with a frame structure of wood and outside with a stone screen built without the use of mortar. Whenever a mound had served its time and began to collapse, the ground had to be levelled and a new mound built. This explains why the remainders of three successively built lines have been found on the southern side of the Castle.

Another inaccessible area of arch-eological excavations is concealed below the Court of Paradise of St. George's Convent. The masonry of older phases of the convent were discovered by I. Borkovský during research work carried out from 1959 to 1962. A wing of the convent building of the late 12th century ran from St. George's Basilica to the north. Its interior was divided into five rooms. The cracks which can clearly be seen in its masonry were evidently caused by the shifting of the foundations down the slope into the gorge of the River Brusnice. In the 13th century a cloister was built-on on to the Romanesque wing of the convent, but only remainders of its foundations have been unearthed. When the Romanesque building had ceased to exist a new cloister was built after the mid-14th century. Its massive masonry with regularly placed supporting pillars demarcated the enlarged Court of Paradise of the convent.

LATIN HYMN BOOK OF 1552

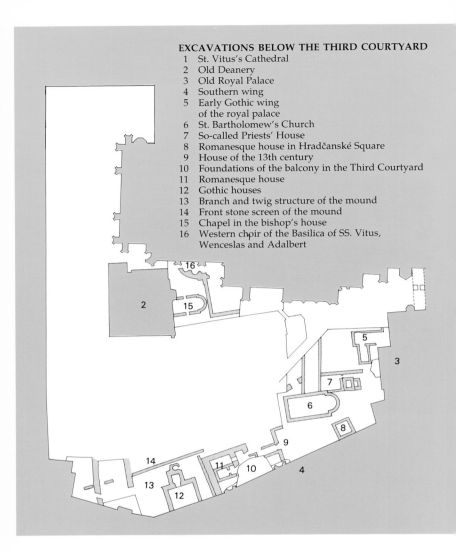

COLLECTIONS

The buildings which are inaccessible to visitors include numerous depositories containing the collection funds of Prague Castle. Works of artistic or historical value do not, however, merely lie around in depositories. Many of them can be seen in the accessible interiors, for example, furniture and paintings in the Old Royal Palace and others in certain expositions (in the Picture Gallery of Prague Castle and in the tower Mihulka). Many serve for the furnishing and decoration of reception and certain official rooms of Prague Castle.

THE ST. VITUS TREASURE

The development of the treasure.

A wholly exceptional position among all the collections of artistic or historical articles at Prague Castle is held by the treasure of St. Vitus's Cathedral. Its age makes it stand out from all others, because its beginnings date back to the time of Prince Václav. The existence of the treasure was documented already in 1069 in connection with the Basilica of St. Vitus, St. Wenceslas and St. Adalbert. Of outstanding importance, however, is also the liturgical value of the

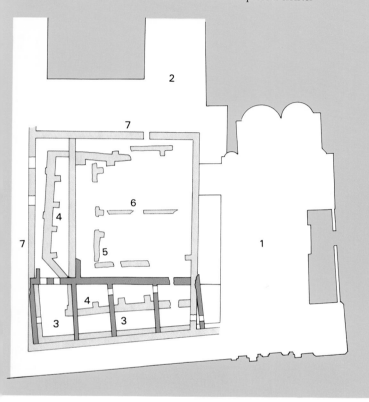

EXCAVATIONS BELOW THE COURT OF PARADISE OF ST. GEORGE'S CONVENT

1. St. George's Basilica
2. Chapel of Our Lady
3. Rooms of the Romanesque convent building
4. Foundations of the Gothic cloister
5. Foundations of the Early Gothic cloister
6. Enclosing wall of the oldest convent
7. Foundations of the present cloister

accumulated relics and liturgical articles along with the high standard of the artistic crafts involved and also – even if in last place – the quality and material value of the precious stones and metals.

One of the oldest of the magnificent reliquaries of the treasure was the valuable casket for the arms of St. Vitus, acquired by Prince Václav himself. Shortly after Václav's death his sword, shield, lances, helmet and chainmail were to become parts of the treasure. After her return from Rome in 973 Boleslav II's sister Mlada enriched the collection with gifts from Pope John XIII and Prince Břetislav I added the relics of St.

Adalbert and the Holy Five Brothers which he brought back with him from his military expedition to Poland. It was thanks to Charles IV, a generous patron of art and a passionate collector of relics, that the treasure enjoyed its greatest period of flourish. Charles acquired relics during his numerous journeys through Europe and added them to the treasure in valuable reliquaries which he had made for them. Thus in 1354, for example, he attended the funeral of his great-uncle Archbishop Balduin at Treves and as the Roman king he had the right to confirm the appointment of a new archbishop, for which a considerably high fee was due to him. Instead of taking it, however, he made it a condition that he would receive one third of the relics from the cathedral at Treves: a part of the relics from the cross of Christ, a part of the stick and shackles of St. Peter and a part of St. Andrew's footwear. In 1354 the first inventory

ARCHBISHOP BREUNER'S
WATER JUG

of the treasure was made and at that time it contained one-hundred-and-fifty items, the list drawn up after the emperor's death containing nearly seven hundred.

The treasure suffered numerous losses during the Hussite wars. True, it did not fall into the hands of plundering troops, but the Emperor Zikmund appropriated a part of the articles and used them to cover his war expenses. A generous donor of the late 15th century was, on the contrary, Vladislav Jagiello. A tradition originated according to which after his coronation the sovereign handed over his garments and perhaps also

other valuable materials for the making of church vestments, which then also became parts of the treasure. When St. Vitus's Cathedral was plundered again in 1619 the greater part of the treasure was once again saved, but a number of articles used during divine services and permanently housed in the cathedral fell victim to the Calvinists. The number of monuments increased in the first third of the 18th century in connection with the sanctification of John Nepomuk (1729). The obligatory contribution of silver to the state mint gave rise to new losses, but the number of articles could once again

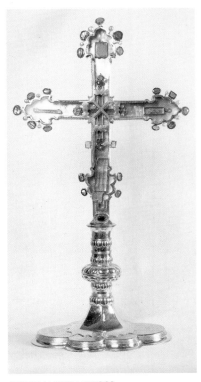

CORONATION CROSS

be increased by means of, for example, the purchase of reliquaries from abolished St. George's Convent. The treasure was partly enriched with numerous gifts from the nobility and the clergy. A group of richly decorated rings and breast crosses came from church dignitaries of the 19th century. Older finds from graves opened during the repairs and completion of St. Vitus's Cathedral were later on also incorporated in the treasure.

In the early 20th century the articles forming the St. Vitus treasure were listed by Bishop A. Podlaha, who published two versions of a catalogue in 1902 and 1903.

Since 1929 the treasure has been installed in the so-called Hilbert's Treasure in the new part of the cathedral, where originally they were also exhibited. In 1961 a selection of the most valuable articles was installed in the Chapel of the Holy Rood in the Second Courtyard, but in 1990 the intallation had to be abolished due to its obsoleteness and inadequate security. Following extensive research carried out from the aspects of art, history and restoration work the question of a new exhibition installation of selected parts of the treasure in the interiors of the Old Royal Palace is being considered.

The most important articles of the treasure

The number of articles forming the St. Vitus treasure now exceeds four hundred. They are an immensely diverse whole. Apart from reliquaries, liturgical articles and vestments for the serving of mass it also contains various monuments, jewels, commemorative coins and medals.

Clearly the oldest items are the parts of the armour of St. Wenceslas, his helmet with a decorative application and a chainmail shirt with a collar of gold rings, preserved from the 9th to 10th centuries. Approximately of the same age is the so-called St. Stephen's sword with a carved bone handle of the 10th century. Two ivory horns with relief decoration also rank in the early Middle Ages.

The Romanesque period is represented by the artistically and technically exceptional lower part of the so-called Milanese bronze candlestick of the mid-12th century, formed by the interwined bodies of a human being and a dragon. A house-shaped reliquary decorated with enamel dates in the same period.

The most outstanding and important articles come from the time of the reign of Charles IV. A crystal jug, originally made from a single big crystal, including the handle, served as a container for the so-called Lord's tablecloth, later kept in a spread state outside the container. The container with a lid for the relic veil of the Virgin Mary is also made of crystal. A nail from Christ's cross was set simply, but effectively in gold. Another reliquary of Christ's martyrdom contains the coronation cross, decorated with rare antique

RELIQUARY BUST OF ST. VITUS

and early medieval cameos. Also set among them on the cross is an exceptionally big sapphire with a carving of Christ's face. The parts of the big procession cross are made of crystal and joined with gilded silver. Pope Urban V's gold cross is decorated with engraved drawings on the front side. One of them portrays the pope handing the mentioned cross to Charles IV.

Another outstanding article – an onyx cup made of one piece of stone – has a gilded mantle bearing an inscription and emblem shields. A number of small, but artistically valuable reliquaries of gilded silver also date from Charles IV's time. Three reliquary busts, the gift of Vladislav Jagiello, have also been preserved from the Late Gothic period. These busts of SS. Wenceslas,

PART OF A DECORATIVE CHAIN

Vitus and Adalbert, hammered from silver plate, are decorated with gilding, real precious stones and their glass imitations. The Kolovrat relics panel with small silver sculptures, precious stones and engravings in mother-of-pearl is also of Late Gothic origin.

Apart from other monuments, the cross of Archbishop Medek, the silver reliquary of the Holy Five Brothers and especially an incomplete set of seventeen superb links of a decorative chain have been preserved from the time of the Emperor Rudolph II. Each one of these links is a separate gold jewel with precious stones, pearls and miniature human and animal figures covered with coloured enamels. These decorations of a rich secular garment have survived thanks to the fact that in the last quarter of the 17th century they became parts of the monstrance of the dean Dlouhoveský. Another exceptionally valuable article – the St. Vitus tabernacle of variously coloured plates of precious stones – was made in the stone-cutting workshop of the Miseroni family, who worked at Prague Castle from Rudolph II's time.

The number of Baroque and Rococo monuments is relative large. Especially worthy of mention are the washbasin of Archbishop Breuner with rich relief decoration, chalices of gilded silver and a gold monstrance, remarkable for its fine, precise working, of 1766.

The artistic craft of the 19th century is well represented by an Empire monstrance which belonged to King Charles X of France and as well as a glass Harrachov monstrance and a bouquet of roses made of gold plate (a gift presented to the Empress Maria Anna, consort of Ferdinand V, by the pope).

The last items to be placed in the treasure are finds from the graves of bishops and rulers, among them, for example, a hat worn by Rudolph II.

THE PICTURE GALLERY OF PRAGUE CASTLE

This designation indicates not only the complex of exhibition rooms on the ground-floor of the northern and the western wing and the works displayed in them, but also the whole collection of paintings of Prague Castle, numbering over two thousand paintings, drawings and graphic sheets of various ages and qualities.

The historical development of the present collection was a long and complicated process. Unfortunately, the legendary collection of paintings of Rudolph II has not been preserved. A small part of it was taken away to Vienna during the Thirty Years' War and the greater part of it was stolen by the Swedes in 1648. The picture gallery was later renewed by Ferdinand III and particularly by his

JACOPO TINTORETTO:
THE FLAGELLATION OF CHRIST

LORENZO LOTTO:
PORTRAIT OF A MUSICIAN

brother, Archduke Leopold Vilém, in the 17th century. From the Twenties of the 18th century the collection of paintings was thinned out as the result of the removal of works to Vienna, later by sales to Saxony and the Josephian auction – and only in a few cases was the loss replaced with new additions. The paintings which were moved from the Picture Gallery to various rooms of the Castle to serve as decorations remained forgotten. It was not until the early Sixties of the present century that they were identified and evaluated in the course of research. The most

PAOLO CALIARI CALLED VERONESE:
PORTRAIT OF THE JEWELLER KÖNIG

important works in the collection were taken over by the new Picture Gallery, opened in 1965. The paintings which are historically connected with the old Picture Gallery of Prague Castle include outstanding works by world-renowned artists. Regarded as the most valuable are Tizian's Toilet of a Young Lady. Tintoretto's Flagellation of Christ or Rubens's The Assembly of the Olympic Gods. Of great value, however, are also the paintings by Hans van Aachen, Domenico Fetti, Bartolomeo Spranger, Paolo Veronese, Jacopo Bassano and his sons Francesco, Leonardo and Gerolamo, and others. Thanks to President Masaryk and his daughter Alice a new picture collection oriented to Czech art of the 18th, 19th and 20th centuries was built-up during the First Republic. Numerous purchases enriched the Castle with works by Petr Brandl, Jan Kupecký, Norbert Grund, Josef Mánes, Adolf Kosárek, Jaroslav Čermák, Václav Brožík, Mikoláš Aleš, Vojtěch Hynais, Antonín Chitussi, Jan Preisler, Antonín Slaviček and many others.

The interiors of the Picture Gallery have been undergoing reconstruction since 1991. Mainly preserved paintings from Leopold Vilém's collection will be concentrated in the new installations.

THE COLLECTION OF FURNITURE AND APPLIED ART

The oldest piece of furniture at Prague Castle is a Renaissance cabinet decorated with surface carving, dated in 1562. It forms a part of the furnishings of the Old Royal Palace and is situated in a room of the New Land Rolls, where there are also other Renaissance and Early Baroque cabinets, tables, chairs and chests. Most of the valuable pieces of historic furniture are used for the furnishing of the reception rooms in the southern and central wings of the Castle. They comprise Baroque, Rococo and Neo-Classical, tarsia and upholstered furniture. A large number of pieces of office furniture in Biedermeier style (commodes, chests-of-drawers, tables and chairs) finds use in the official rooms. A part of the furniture manufactured after designs by the architect Josip Plečnik has been preserved in the apartment of President T. G. Masaryk.

Numerous period clocks, mirrors, oriental vases and small sculptures are particularly remarkable among the articles of applied art. Most of the especially valuable ones among them decorate the reception rooms.

THE COLLECTION OF HISTORIC TEXTILE

This collection comprises tapestries, carpets and textile from burial finds. Apart from several modern pieces, the gobelin collection contains about forty works of the 17th and 18th centuries. Of the greatest value among them are the Blue Moon cycle (produced by a manufactory at La Malgrance in France) and the Anthony and Cleopatra cycle (woven in Brussels in the 17th century. Unfortunately, both cycles are incomplete. Likewise from Brussels is a series of months with big, winged female figures. Gobelins and valuable Persian and other oriental carpets find use particularly for the decoration of the reception rooms. Textile monuments found in the course of archeological research cannot, on the contrary, be permanently displayed and, furthermore, exacting conditions have to be fulfilled with regard to their storage. The fund of historical textile includes fragments of materials from the royal graves. Outstanding among these are the

CASTINGS OF STONE EMBLEMS

recently restored dalmatic of Václav IV and the almost complete burial apparel of Rudolph II. Equally noteworthy are the parts of the garments of the Hapsburgs buried in the Royal Mausoleum and fragments from the graves of bishops or the abbesses of St. George's Convent. One of the oldest materials (of the 10th century) was raised from the grave of St. Ludmila during archeological research in 1981.

CASTINGS, DESIGNS AND MODELS

Plaster castings enable the study of details whose originals are preserved in places difficult of access. However, they are not intended exclusively for

MODEL OF PRAGUE CASTLE IN THE ROMANESQUE PERIOD

art historians and other specialists. Many castings have originated for exhibition purposes. For visitors they can partly compensate for the fact that some interiors or places are inaccessible and that it is not possible for them to reach certain details. This applies, for example, in the case of the busts in the inner triforium in the cathedral and of other sculptures from the decoration of its supporting system, exhibited on the Gothic floor of the Old Royal Palace. The castings of the sculptures of the outer triforium, and not only these, are of great value for restoration work. Very often they portray the original in a better state than it was later at the time of its restoration. The last cas-

FRAGMENT OF TERRACOTTA FROM PERNŠTEJN PALACE

tings, produced from a part of the stucco decorations of the Spanish Hall, preserved from the time of Rudolph II, are also intended for exhibition purposes.

The collection of designs and models contains works created for various competitions and projects. Among the interesting documents forming the collection there are in particular designs of reliefs for the western bronze door of the cathedral, models of gargoyles for the cathedral and J. Plečnik's model of an unrealized monolith for the Garden of Paradise. The architectural models represent reconstructions of the form of the Castle in various periods (in the 10th century, in the Romanesque period and at the time during which the Luxembourgs ruled the country) and the present form of individual buildings.

THE STONE COLLECTION

The stone collection, housed in several depositories, contains and affords protection to architectural elements or their fragments, found in excavations or during buildings works, or originals replaced with copies on the spot.

The largest number of stone details comes from St. Vitus's Cathedral: fragments of pinnacles and window traceries, two coping stones, a number of fragments from the original decoration of the interior of the Golden Portal (after which they were constructed) and originals of provincial emblems from the southern spiral staircase. The stone collection also contains a number of Romanesque capitals and fragments of decorated columns from St. Vitus's Basilica, a whole vault rib from the Gothic period, large groups of terracotta details from the Renaissance period and fragments of sculptures from the Baroque period.

ARCHEOLOGICAL FINDS

There are several depositories of archeological finds at the Castle and all of them are full. Every year since 1925 systematic research of the Castle has brought – and continues to bring – more and more gains which enrich former ones.

The fund of finds is very varied. Splinters of various vessels prevail among them. Also contained here are fragments of glass from window panes and vessels, various metal articles, coins, products made of bone and, uniquely, also jewellery. The most valuable finds include gold jewels from graves on the area of the Pheasantry of the late 9th to the late 10th century, a glass, so-called Arab cup of the 13th century, a group of vessels of the 12th and the early 13th century found in the so-called Romanesque well in the basement of the southern wing, richly decorated majolica and gilded Renaissance tiles from Rožmberk Palace, found in the Garden on the Ramparts, and a gold ring from the same research.

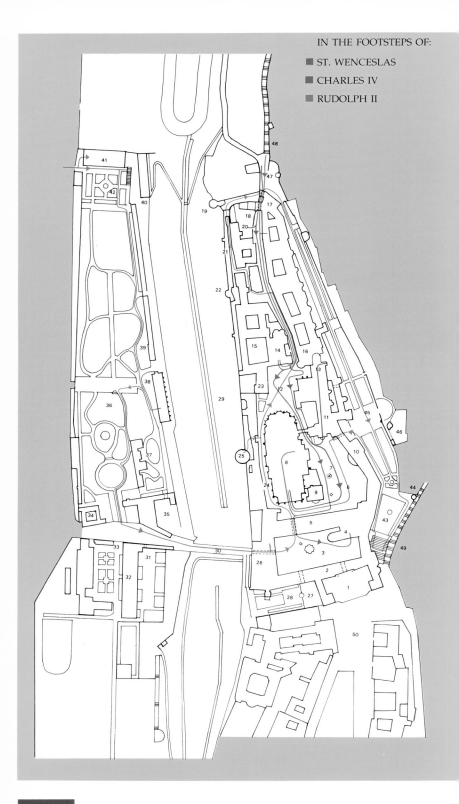

IN THE FOOTSTEPS OF HISTORIC PERSONAGES

IN THE FOOTSTEPS OF PRINCE VÁCLAV

Not many tangible witnesses of the period of Prince Václav and with a direct relation to his person at Prague Castle could be preserved. However, in view of the fact that St. Wenceslas (Václav) is one of the most important personages of early Czech history and the most highly esteemed of the provincial saints we come across a number of portraits of him on the whole Castle area.

Let us set out in his traces from the area in front of the eastern gate of the Castle, from the place called Opyš. The wooden gate in the enclosing wall between the Old Castle. Steps and the sloping street Na Opyši leads to the St. Wenceslas Vineyard. This easternmost part of the rocky Castle headland, which has never been a part of the fortified territory of the Castle, is traditionally considered to be the vineyard where, according to a legend, St. Wenceslas cultivated the vine. According to the legend he allegedly "made haste, picked the grapes and pressing them with his own hands poured the wine into jugs and preserved it for the need of his devotions". He also baked hosts himself from flour prepared with his own hands: "At harvest time he used to walk in his fields in the silence of the deep night and sowed wheat, carrying it home on his own shoulders, grinding it on a hand mill and, as a baker and duke in one person, sieved the flour and then went for water, also at night, with the words: In the name of the Father, the Son and the Holy Spirit".

Let us now pass through the gate to the Castle and walk up Jiřská Street round Lobkowicz Palace. Some of the windows on the first floor belong to the palace chapel, consecrated to St. Wenceslas. The altar painting of St. Wenceslas with angels dates in the 18th century and is allegedly the work of one of Brandl's successors. In St. George's Basilica we can see the cretaceous marly limestone tomb of Václav's father Vratislav I, supplemented with a painted wooden extension. An empty grave hole hollowed out in the rocky outcrop in the chapel below the southern steeple is believed to be the place where St. Wenceslas most likely had the bodily remains of his grandmother, Princess Ludmila, transferred from Tetín, laid to rest. Only later was the saint's grave moved to St. Ludmila's Chapel, where we can also see a portrait of St. Wenceslas in the paintings on the vault of the late 16th century and on the side slab of the tomb of the mid-14th century. Various portraits which originated several centuries after the death of Prince Václav tell us, however, very little about his real likeness and his armour or garments. The author of the legend of the 10th century about St. Wenceslas tells us that he "dressed continuously in a woollen robe on his bare body like a monk, but, covered on top with the most beautiful princely robes, he shone before God and the people".

Another idea of the appearance of Prince Václav is afforded by the statue of 1880 on the corner of the Neo-Gothic New Deanery in the square U svatého Jiří. On glancing up at the choir part of the cathedral we are reminded that a bust of St. Wenceslas is a part of the gallery of provincial saints on the outer triforium. We shall now continue along the cathedral to the Third Courtyard. From here we can see not only a copy of the well-known Gothic statue (situated on the baldachin on the pillars above St. Wenceslas's Chapel), but also the figure of St. Wenceslas among the other saints of the kingdom in the lower part of the mosaic on the Golden Portal.

One of the bells on the big steeple, dating in 1542, bears the name Václav. However, St. Wenceslas is also brought to mind by a relief on the biggest bell here, Zikmund, of 1549. The projection in the south-western corner of the Third Courtyard is connected with the building of the court chapel consecrated to St. Wenceslas, situated on the first floor of the palace from 1644. It is now recalled by the so-called Octagon in the row of reception rooms. Another statue, this time by J. J. Bendl, can be seen on the corner of the Old Deanery. The inscription on its pedestal tells us that it originated in 1662. We could also find the figure of St. Wenceslas (along with St. Vitus) in the Chapel of the Holy Rood in the Second Courtyard, specifically in a painting by F. X. Balko of the period after the mid-18th century.

The largest number of portraits of St. Wenceslas is concentrated in St. Vitus's Cathedral. Scenes from his life formed the theme for the decoration of the right-hand (southern) bronze door in the western façade. One of the most outstanding in the interior of the cathedral is the portrait on a window in the New Archbishop's Chapel (A. Mucha, 1931), similarly as those in a carving on the door of the Choir Chapel below the music choir (1639), on one of the pillars at the point of intersection of the main and transverse naves (a gilded wooden statue, F. Preisse, 1696), in the big composition of three choir windows (M. Švabinský, 1945–1948), on the altar in St. John Nepomuk's Chapel (a silver bust, 1699) and on the spiral sprinkler in front of St. Wenceslas's Chapel (a bronze statue, K. Dvořák, 1922).

However, we are reminded of St. Wenceslas also by other motifs and places. On the tombs of the Přemyslid princes in the choir chapels there is the St. Wenceslas female eagle, the original emblem of the Czech principality. By the spiral staircase leading to Hilbert's treasury it is impossible not to recall the monuments deposited in the St. Vitus treasure. They are a helmet with a decorated nose shield and chain armour with a loose collar decorated with gold rings. Of St. Wenceslas's reliquaries mention must be made at least of the bust of gilded silver of 1486, the gift of Vladislav Jagiello. Also housed in Hilbert's treasury is the skull of St. Wenceslas in an ostentatious Art Nouveau arrangement after J. Fanta (1929).

On the area of the archeological excavations below the floor of the cathedral a small part of the foundation masonry of the northern apse of St. Vitus's Rotunda, founded by Prince Václav, can be seen. The prince was a passionate supporter of Christianity at the time when "superstitious pagan rituals had not yet been plucked from their roots; however, because he esteemed the Lord, showed the way of truth to those who had gone astray and preserved humility, patience, moderateness and love" – Christians "flew to him like bees to a hive". During the reign of Charles IV St. Wenceslas's Chapel with the grave of St. Wenceslas was built above the southern apse of the original rotunda. In 1911 the grave was subjected to research by the architect K. Hilbert and the sanctifying bishop A. Podlaha. The remainder of a Gothic tomb of sandstone ashlars with hewn-out, empty beds for polished precious stones was discovered below the marble panelling of the tomb. After the disassembly of the tomb a walled-up grave was found below the slab on the level of the old paving. Inside it there was a big lead chest containing earth transferred from the original grave. Only then was a small lead chest with the remains of St. Wenceslas placed in it.

St. Wenceslas's Chapel has painted scenes from the St. Wenceslas legend on the upper parts of the walls. They date in the early 16th century.

The central scene, to which the greatest space is devoted, shows the recenption of St. Wenceslas as the imperial elector at the Diet in Regensburg. A legend describes it as follows: "The blessed Václav, summoned to the imperial court, was received with respect by the emperor and the princes and, invited to the imperial Diet and Council, he hesitated to arrive in the morning after his night's work and labour spent in vigils and prayers, so that the emperor and the princes thought that he was conceited and lazy. And so the emperor and the princes decided that if he arrived late they would not pay honour to him. However, as soon as the blessed Václav joined the ranks of the emperor and princes, the emperor saw that he was led by angels and that the brightest glitter of a golden cross glowed on his forehead . . . They then invited him to order and request anything he wanted. He saluted the martyr who the emperor gave him. When he brought him to Prague, he built a church in honour of this illustrious martyr". A beautiful Gothic statue of St. Wenceslas, the most outstanding and important sculptured work from Parler's workshop at Prague Castle, stands on the cornice above the altar table. An enormous bronze candlestick from the workshop of H. Vischer, a gift of the Old Town brewers of 1532, represents another sculptured portrait of the saint. The murder of St. Wenceslas at Stará Boleslav is depicted in a panel painting by the monographist IW (1543). At the time of Charles IV a Romanesque knocker was transferred to St. Wenceslas's Chapel (on the northern door). For a long time it was believed that Prince Václav held it during the last moments of his life. This is only a legend, however. The knocker originated about two hundred years later.

Leading from the interior of the chapel is the legendary door with seven locks leading to the Crown Chamber with the crown of Czech kings, which from the beginning was consecrated to St. Wenceslas as "the heir to the Czech land". According to the wish of Charles IV it was to rest permanently on his head, by which was evidently meant a reliquary for the saint's skull in the form of a bust.

VIEW OF THE INTERIOR OF ST. WENCESLAS'S CHAPEL ▶

IN THE FOOTSTEPS OF CHARLES IV

Our walk through Prague Castle of Charles IV once again begins at the place called Opyš in front of the eastern gate. The Black Tower, the only one of all the towers of the Romanesque fortification system which is still visible, rises next to it. At the time of Charles IV it had a roof of thickly gilded lead plate and its glitter, which could be seen a long distance away, welcomed the numerous visitors to the Castle. After his return from France in 1333 Charles occupied the neighbouring closed area of the Burgrave's Residence, still as the margrave of Moravia, until the reconstruction of the heavily damaged royal palace was completed. It was also here that the event involving a goblet, which Charles himself described in his autobiography (Vita Caroli), took place: Once in winter he returned with his friend Bušek of Velhartice from Křivoklát Castle in the late evening and they both went to bed in the Burgrave's house. However, during the night they were woken up by unusual sounds. Although the doors and the windows were closed and no one could be seen, loud steps could be heard in the room. It was as though one of the goblets on the table had been knocked over by someone and then thrown against the wall by an unknown force.

King Charles certainly also used to walk from the Burgrave's Residence to St. George's Basilica. St. George's Convent and the church were reconstructed during his reign, but nowadays only traces of that ancient activity can be seen. Through a grille in St. Ludmila's Chapel it is possible to see a tomb whose sculptured decoration (the upper slab with the figure of St. Ludmila and the side slabs with the small figures of saints) comes just from Charles's time as do the large pointed windows in the western façade of the basilica, visible, however, only when viewed form within.

From Jiřské Square we shall now view the oldest part of St. Vitus's Cathedral. On Sunday 21 November, 1344 the square witnessed the solemn laying of the foundation stone of the cathedral. In front of the eyes of the assembled lords, knights and clergy King John of Luxembourg descended into the ditch for the foundations with his sons Charles and John and the archbishop Arnošt of Pardubice for the memorable ceremony. The lower choir chapels of the cathedral were built by Matthias of Arras until 1352, the building from the gallery above the chapels and higher being the work of Peter Parler.

Charles IV had the Royal Palace rebuilt after the model of the palaces of French kings, with which he himself was well-acquainted. Still visible of the building is a part of the arcades in the northern court of the palace and some rooms on the Gothic floor on this level. At the time of Charles IV the area of the Vladislav Hall of the present was occupied by a reception floor with a great hall: to be seen of it on the walls are revealed details of large windows and visible in the southern wall is a part of the arch of the bay-windowed chapel consecrated to Our Lady. Next to the entrance, on the Riders' Staircase, a part of a large portal from Charles's time has been preserved. In those days the main entrance to the great hall was situated just here. From the observation place affording a view of the city we can see the original large windows of All Saints' Church, made smaller during the reconstruction in 1580. At Charles IV's time they took up the whole width of the wall between the supporting pillars and they were higher, similarly as the vault, whose remainders can be seen in the truss above the present vault.

When gazing into the Garden on the Ramparts we must bring to mind Charles's considerable improvement of the southern fortifications. The chronicler Beneš Krabice of Weitmile tells us in respect of the year 1370 that the emperor noticed the inadequate fortifications of the Castle on the side facing the town and therefore had a big ditch dug. In actual fact, however, the southern parkan wall was built at that time a ditch being dug and mounds heaped in front of it.

In the Third Courtyard, which had two elevations during the reign of Charles IV, let us first notice the vertical band of blind windows in the façade of the central wing next to the entrance to the tunnel. Concealed here is the Romanesque masonry of the huge White Tower, which, similarly as the Black Tower, Charles IV had provided with a gilded roof. The ceremonial entrance to St. Vitus's Cathedral is next to the great steeple, which was built after Charles's death. The area above the three entrance arches is covered by a large mosaic The Last Judgement, a work of 1370 to 1371 executed "in the Greek manner, a magnificent and very costly work", as a contemporary chronicler tells. The glass cubes of the mosaic were evidently manufactured by a domestic glassworks, but from the very beginning up to the present it has been marked by a technological error causing its bad state. The kneeling figures of Charles IV and his consort Elizabeth of Pomerania can be seen on the sides of the central arch, below the group of patron saints of the Czech Kingdom.

A statue of Charles IV can be seen on the western façade of the cathedral (S. Sucharda, 1908), while a relief scene portraying the visit of the emperor to the building of the cathedral can be observed along with other scenes from the history of the cathedral on the bronze entrance door.

The most authentic monuments of Charles IV's time are situated inside the cathedral. These are the Gothic wall paintings and the cretaceous marly limestone tombs of the Přemyslid princes and kings in the choir chapels. On the basis of the personal order of Charles IV the tombs were made by the Parler workshop and Beneš Krabice transferred the remains of the rulers from the old church to them. Modern research has made it possible to ascertain in detail how they were built. The tomb itself is always empty and stands on a thick sandstone slab closing the grave hollow proper. A simple casket made of boards hammered with nails and containing bones wrapped in white linen and a lead plate with an identification plate was placed in it.

Mention must be made of Charles's merit regarding the St. Vitus treasure. The contemporary chronicler František Pražský wrote that "none of the other kings of this kingdom raised, enriched and honoured the said Prague Church in such an excellent and magnificent way". History shows that this evaluation is correct not only as regards the period of reign of Charles IV, as the chronicler said, but also with respect to the following period. The most costly and the artistically most valuable articles really date in Charles's time: the coronation cross (originally a part of the Karlštejn treasure), the crystal procession cross, the crystal jug, the onyx goblet and the gold cross of Pope Urban V – it would be difficult to find their like.

A finger of St. Nicholas, with which an event recorded by several chroniclers is connected, is deposited in one of the numerous reliquaries. The event in question is the emperor's visit in 1353 to the St. Francis "convent of virgins", i.e., to the present St. Agnes's Convent. He manifested interest in a part of the relics kept here and cut off a piece of the dried-up finger of St. Nicholas. To the amazement of the emperor and his entourage a drop of fresh blood appeared on the old relic. When Charles returned to the convent several days later and had the cut-off part of the finger returned to its original place, both parts of the finger joined-up to form a whole . . .

The portrait busts of the inner triforium of the cathedral are an important monument recalling Charles IV. Among them are busts of the imperial family, especially of Charles IV, and all his four consorts. The first of them, Blanche of Valois, who he married in 1323, provided him with two daughters. After their marriage in 1348 his second consort, Anne of the Palatinate, gave birth to a son Václav, but he died as a small child. Anna Svídnická, who he married in 1353, was the most beautiful princess in Europe at that time and their marriage brought forth a son Václav, later King Václav IV. The head of Charles's last consort – Elizabeth of Pomerania – indicates the strength of this empress due to its size. The chronicler Beneš Krabice witnessed several times with his own eyes how Elizabeth broke a horseshoe, swords and weighty knives and tore armour (evidently chain armour) from top to bottom with her own hands. Her strength surpassed that of even the strongest man, but she demonstrated it only when Charles IV asked her to do so. In all six children were born to Charles and Elizabeth, among them Zikmund, later the king of hungary and the Czech king and Roman emperor.

Although the busts of the triforium of the cathedral are rather official portraits, anthropological research of the respective skulls has shown that they most likely correspond to the real likeness of those portrayed.

The conformity of other portraits of Charles IV, some of which show his bent figure, is also remarkable. The anthropologist E. Vlček, who carried out research of the emperor's remains when his coffin was opened in the royal tomb in 1976 and is the last to do so, explains Charles's hunchbacked figure as the result of a spinal injury. A whole number of healed injuries was found on Charles IV's skeleton. Along with the emperor's robust athletic figure they witness the facts that Charles was a real medieval knight, that he took part in numerous battles and that he participated in many touraments. These likings (and his bent for garments in the fashion of the time) gained him a reprimand from Pope Clement VI.

Apart from other things, Charles's contemporaries also recorded the fact that when giving an audience he cut rods, but listened attentively as he did so. His replies were brief, but to the point. His statements were written down by three scribes in order that they might have time to record them literally.

Charles IV devoted the greatest care to the decoration of St. Wenceslas's Chapel. St. Wenceslas held first place among the provincial saints and Charles always showed special respect for him and even wrote one of the verses of the legend about the saint himself. He regarded the chapel itself as the most important part of the cathedral and had it decorated in a wholly exceptional way. The polished precious stones are meant to recall the walls and towers of heavenly Jerusalem and the wall painting the martyrdom of Jesus Christ. The lower part of the walls has been preserved practically in its original state of Charles's time. He himself and Elizabeth of Pomerania are portrayed on the sides of The Crucifixion.

Charles's portrait – a modern one – can also be seen on the large window of the high choir, where he is depicted as the founder of the cathedral with a model of its building in his hands, and also on the southern window in the transverse nave, among the group of Czech kings.

Our walk in the footsteps of the emperor and king Charles IV ends with a glance into the royal tomb. The sovereign, called the Father of His Country, lies in the middle sarcophagus. In accordance with his will his rich robes were removed after the ostentatious burial ceremonies, following which he was buried modestly in the simple habit worn by a Minorite monk.

THE ENCHANTING ATMOSPHERE OF THE GOLDEN LANE

IN THE FOOTSTEPS OF RUDOLPH II

Rudolph II resided in Prague from 1583. Our walk in his footsteps begins in the Royal Summer Palace, which had been wholly completed before his arrival in Prague. Thus he could not only admire it, but also make full use of it. Rudolph had a part of his art collection, renowned all over Europe, installed in it. It has been proved historically that several bronze sculptures, in particular a group of statues Mercury and Psyché, now in Paris, once stood here. The use of the building for art purposes is brought to mind by one of the wall paintings on the first floor of the palace. It portrays the emperor inspecting the torso of a Classical statue of Illioneus. The painting dates in the 19th century. From the eastern side of the arcade and the terrace the emperor was able to watch games and perhaps also tournaments taking place on the open tilting-ground on the site of Chotek Park (Chokové sady) of the present.

From the Royal Summer Palace we shall now continue through the Royal Garden (Královská zahrada), which Rudolph enriched with several buildings and some new species of plants. A structure for fig trees and the cultivation and protection in winter of exotic plants, which were a great fashion in Renaissance gardens, originated below the summer palace. In the colder part of the year they were removed to the structure for fig trees, covered with a roof which could be disassembled and a thick layer of what was probably straw to secure thermal insulation.

The same function was fulfilled by another structure by the path on the edge of the ditch – an orangery. However, its present appearance is the result of its reconstruction in the Sixties of the present century.

By walking along the side of the orangery we come to the Big Ball-games Hall, built at the time of Rudolph's predecessors, but widely used during his reign. The ball game which the court society played here was similar to tennis and the emperor was fond of watching the players in secret. However, he could satisfy his commonly known bent for arriving and remaining unobserved mainly in the Small Ball-games Hall, which no longer exists. It stood near the street U Prašného mostu, which Rudolph reached, without being seen, by means of a "secret" passage whose existence was common knowledge. It was situated in the upper, roofed deck of the bridge and in the buildings round the present Stable Court at the entrance to the Royal Garden, where a part of it has been preserved.

We must not overlook the Lion Court in the north-western corner of the garden. It was built in Rudolph's time on the site of an older menagerie. Apart from lions, which had been bred here already previously as the emblem animals of the kingdom, visitors could at that time also see other beasts of prey. The emperor used the leopard among them for hunting. He founded an enclosure for deer in the natural gorge of the River Brusnice between the Castle and the Royal Garden. True, we can imagine Stag Ditch full of game, but without tall trees. For defence reasons the slopes of the ditches and mounds were kept in good view.

Rudolph II enlarged the complex of gardens from the path of access also in westerly direction. Here a pheasantry for "Indian" birds imported from America and a pond for the breeding of fish and water fowl originated. The pond has been preserved in an almost unchanged form to the present. Water was conducted to it by means of piping made of bored tree trunks. A part of it has been found during archeological research.

We shall now make our way to the Castle itself by walking along the embankment which filled the gorge in front of the northern gate and covered the one-time bridge. The safety of the Emperor Rudolph was guarded by two hundred men of his personal guard, one hundred of them being foot soldiers and one hundred horsemen.

In the northern façade, which we can see from the bridge, a row of high windows of the first floor betrays the Spanish Hall and, in the receding part of the façade on the left, the Rudolph Gallery. On the ground-floor, below the ceremonial rooms, there are long, vaulted stables along both sides of the entrance which were partly built by Rudolph and used for the stabling of his valuable, mainly Spanish horses. The upper rooms are seen by visitors only very rarely. They are reached through an entrance in the central wing between the Second and Third Courtyards. Approximately on the site of the present staircase leading to the upper floors there once stood the medieval Bishop's Tower, provided with an observation terrace and renamed the Mathematical Tower at Rudolph's time. On the first floor of this wing there is a wide corridor where the emperor's "art chamber", a collection of works of an artistic craft character and curiosities which enjoyed great renown, was situated. Rudolph had a picture gallery in the similarly situated room on the next floor. A wide corridor leads to the entrance to Rudolph's gallery, which was built towards the end of the emperor's reign and served for the display of paintings.

The neighbouring Spanish Hall was intended for large sculptural works. Proof exists that Adrian de Vries exhibited his above-lifesize mythological sculptures of fired clay and stucco here. Many of the original stucco wall decorations have been preserved here. They include the emperor's monogram (a crowned R with the order of the Golden Fleece) above the central window.

Apart from paintings by old masters, purchased all over Europe, the emperor's magnificent gallery also contained numerous works by then new artists, painted directly for Rudolph. The care which he devoted to the purchase of works of art is documented by the example of Dürer's The Feast of the Rosaries. Purchased in Venice, the painting was carefully wrapped in several protective layers and throughout the whole journey strong men carried it hung on a rod in order to prevent it from being damaged (the route ran across the Alps!).

An unbelievable wealth of works of an artistic craft nature filled the emperor's art chamber. According to the testimonies of his contemporaries and a preserved inventory Rudolph accumulated vessels carved of amber and ivory, jewellery and medals. Works of unusual natural materials (coconuts, shells, bezoars, animals' horns, etc.) were a great fashion at Rudolph's time. They were set in gold and silver, but attention was also aroused by numerous natural curiosities, stuffed rare animals, exotic folk products from Africa, Asia and America, antique vessels and even mummies from Ancient Egypt.

And yet another interior has preserved its almost authentic appearance since Rudolph's time. We would find it – if it were accessible to the public, of course – on the second floor of the Romanesque White Tower. This is built-in into the massif of the central wing and we can recognize it only from the Third Courtyard according to its blind windows.

It has a richly decorated vault with a wall painting of the god Herma and the goddess Athene in the central circular field.

From the central wing we now continue through Vikářská Street to the Powder Tower (Mihulka), where alchemists worked during Rudolph's reign. In the vicinity of the tower, behind the Vikárka restaurant, there is a long building known as the Foundry where a number of bronze statues as well as bells, etc. originated at that time.

After crossing the square called U svatého Jiří we enter Jiřská Street and pass by the green façade of the Institute of Gentlewomen. At Rudolph's time, however it was still Rožmberk Palace, which the emperor gained in 1600. After walking round house No. 10, in which the emperor's court painter Hans von Aachen lived, we come to the Golden Lane (Zlatá ulička), usually incorrectly connected with legends about alchemists. Nevertheless, it is connected with the person of Rudolph II – in 1597 he allotted this sector of the fortification wall to the castle marksmen in order that they might build modest dwellings here. A special decree was issued in this connection.

If we continue further and pass through the eastern gate at Opyš we can return through the southern gardens along the façade of the Castle as far as the Garden of Paradise. Here, in the westernmost part, Rudolph had his private bath and an aviary. The so-called Buglers' Tower, whose appearance is now known to us only from old engravings, also used to stand here. When glancing up at the Castle we can see on the level of the second and third floors the place where the emperor had his private chambers (the so-called "Sommerhaus") built.

In the centre of the southern gardens let us now ascend the Bulls' Staircase to the Third Courtyard, directly opposite the steeple of St. Vitus's Cathedral. Rudolph II is brought to mind by the gilded ornamental grille covering the biggest bell of the cathedral and a black-and-gold tablet with the imperial monogram.

Our visit to the monuments of Rudolph II ends at the cathedral where we shall take a look into the royal tomb. Here, below an ostentatious marble mausoleum, which was completed during Rudolph's reign, the emperor himself was laid to eternal rest. His tin, partly painted coffin of 1612 stands in the centre at the rear.

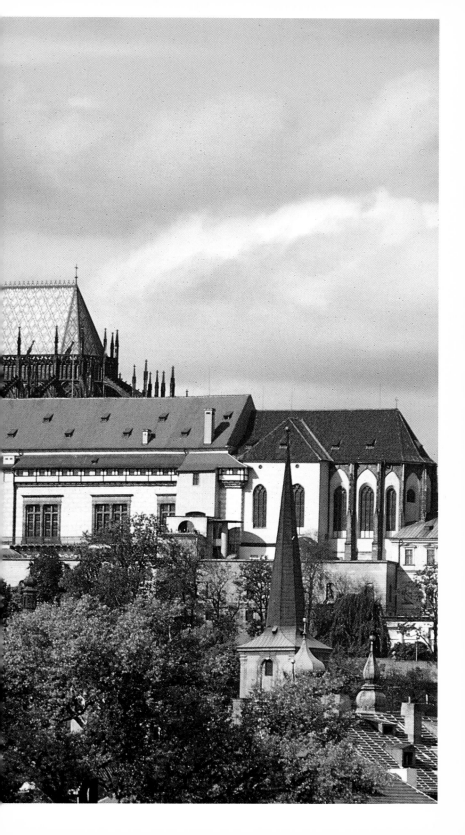

PRACTICAL INFORMATION FOR VISITORS TO PRAGUE CASTLE

Visiting times

The area of Prague Castle is open daily throughout the whole year, in the summer season from April to October from 5am to midnight and in the winter season from November to March from 5am to 11pm. The buildings which can be visited are also accessible daily, always from 9am to 5pm in the summer season and from 5am to 4pm in the winter season with the exception of St. Vitus's Cathedral, which is open only in favourable weather from April to October. The castle gardens are open in the same period and they are accessible from 10am to 6pm.

Prague Castle is one of the most frequented cultural-historical monuments in Prague and as a result its buildings are literally flooded with visitors in the main tourist season. This applies particularly between 10.30am to 12.30 pm and between 2pm and 4pm. When planning the time of the start of your tour of inspection of the Castle you are advised to bear this fact in mind.

Admission tickets, guides, Information Centre

In order to be able to enter accessible buildings it is neccesary to have an admission ticket. This can be bought in all of them or at the Information Centre in the Chapel of the Holy Rood in the Second Courtyard.

No admission charge is made for children of up to 6 years of age.

Half charges are payable in the case of children of 6 to 16 years of age and students.

An admission ticketss enables entry to the marked buildings:
1. St. Vitus's Cathedral – the royal tomb, choir and steeple.
2. The Old Royal Palace
3. St. George's Basilica
4. The Power Tower – Mihulka

All the gardens of Prague Castle can be entered free of charge.

If you decide to tour the area of the Castle with a guide we recommend you to use the Castle guide services. Fully qualified employees are ready to accompany you individually or in groups and to provide commentaries in foreign languages. Their services can be gained directly at the Information Centre, or ordered in advance (tel. 33 37 33 68). The employees of the Information Centre will also answer your questions and provide you with basic information material and publications about Prague Castle. The Information Centre is open in the same periods as the accessible buildings, i.e, daily from 9am to 5pm (or 4pm).

How to get to Prague Castle

By car

If you travel by car you will have only one possibility of parking on weekdays and that is at Pohořelec, in the vicinity of Loretánské Square. By walking along Loretánské Street you will arrive at the main entrance to the Castle via Hradčanské Square. This will not take you more than 15 minutes and on your way you can admire a number of other monuments, for example, Černín Palace, the Loretto with a carillon, Schwarzenberg Palace, the Archbishop's Palace and Šternberk Palace with an exposition of the National Gallery from its collections of European art. – At weekends you can also use the U Prašného mostu car park situated in close proximity to the stop of tram No. 22. From here you will now walk along the street of the same name, passing the Riding-school of Prague Castle and the entrance to the Royal Garlen via Stag Ditch and arriving directly at the northern gate leading to the Second Courtyard.

By the underground railway and tram

Visitors who do not possess their own transport means appreciate the advantageous connection between the underground railway and the tram system. The <u>A line of the underground railway</u> runs to Prague Castle. It is best to get out at the <u>Malostranská</u> station and then continue by <u>tram No. 22</u> (in Bílá hora direction) to the Pražský hrad stop.

On foot

Physically abler visitors may choose to reach the Castle by <u>walking up the old Castle Steps</u> from the Malostranská station of the underground railway. A unique view of the city from the Na Opyši observation place, situated in front of the entrance to the Castle through the Black Tower, will reward them for their efforts. The Castle can also be reached by means of the so-called <u>New Castle Steps</u> which in turn can be reached from Malostranská Square.

Themes for a sightseeing tour

A selection of buildings to be visited at Prague Castle and decisions concerning the amount of time to spend at them depend on the interest and time possibilities of every visitor. For those visiting the Castle for the first time we are offering several basic sightseeing variants along with the approximate time necessary for their realization.

1. <u>A route taking 1.5 hours</u>

The route of this sightseeing tour begins in St. Vitus's Cathedral, where we visit the Neo-Gothic part and the choir surrounding the high altar, continues with a glance into St. Wenceslas's Chapel and then, after descending a flight of steps, a visit to the tomb of Czech kings. From the cathedral we make our way through the Golden Portal or the main entrance to the Third Courtyard and enter the Old Royal Palace. Here we visit the Vladislav Hall, the Czech Office, the rooms of the New Land Rolls and the Old Diet and then descend the Riders' Staircase and go out into Jiřské Square. From here we make our way to the opposite St. George's Basilica and, after inspecting its interior, turn left down Jiřská Street and turn off into the Golden Lane. From here it is possible to continue below the Black Tower to the Old Castle Steps, which will take us direct to the Malostranská station of the underground railway.

2. A route taking 2 hours

We extend the previous route by making a more detailed tour of the Old Royal Palace. We visit the rooms of Charles IV on the Gothic floor and can also descend from the Vladislav Hall to the newly opened Theresian Wing.

3. A route taking 3 hours

In this case tours of the interiors of the mentioned buildings are supplemented with a walk through the castle gardens. The southern gardens of Prague Castle can be entered from Hradčanské Square (the New Castle Steps), from the Third Courtyard by means of the so-called Bulls' Staircase by the Old Royal Palace, or from the Old Castle Steps in the vicinity of the Black Tower. Entrance can be gained to the Royal Garden from the street U Prašného mostu, or from the Royal Summer Palace.

4. A one-day sightseeing tour

If you wish a devote a whole day to Prague Castle you can extend a visit to its monuments by devoting some time to other sights on its area. Apart from short-term exhibitions organized in various buildings, we recommend a visit to the very valuable permanent

Services on the area of Prague Castle

Restaurants and cafés
The Poet Café – in the Garden on the Bastion
Vikárka – a restaurant and wine bar – Vikářská Street
U kanovníků (At the Canons) – a restaurant – Vikářská Street
Bonal – refreshments – the Golden Lane
Café terrace – Jiřská Street, Lobkowicz Palace

Post Office – telephone, fax
The Third Courtyard

Currency exchange offices
The Information Centre in the Chapel of the Holy Rood in the Second Courtyard and in Vikářská Street.

Castle police station
Vikářská Street (can also be used in the case of losses and pocket thefts).

First Aid
In urgent cases turn to the employees of the Information Centre, who will arrange medical assistance.

Sale of literature, postcards and souvenirs
The shop in the Information Centre in the Chapel of the Holy Rood in the Second Courtyard,
the Green Room (Zelená světnice) shop in the antechamber of the Old Royal Palace,
the stylish shops in the historic little houses in the Golden Lane.

Public toilets
By the Riding-school of Prague Castle on the right-hand side of the main entrance to St. Vitus's Cathedral, the Old Royal Palace, Jiřská Street, the Garden on the Ramparts, near the Royal Summer Palace.

exhibitions – the exposition from the collections of old Czech art of the National Gallery in St. George's Convent and the historical exposition of the National Museum in Lobkowicz Palace where, apart from other things, copies of the Czech coronation jewels can be seen.

What should also be seen

The ceremony of the changing of the Castle Guard with the handing-over of the standard of the president of the Czech Republic takes place every day at noon in the First Courtyard.

Changing of the guard at the gates of Prague Castle takes place on the stroke of every hour.

The present ceremony was introduced in 1990 along with the new uniforms of the Castle Guard (designed by T. Pištěk). Since then fanfares are played by the orchestra of the Castle Guard from the windows of the western wing above the First Courtyard when the ceremony of the changing of the guard takes place. They were composed by M. Kocáb.

Religious services are held in St. Vitus's Cathedral regularly every Sunday morning.

Promenade concerts take place in the Garden on the Ramparts every Saturday from 10am from May to October.

Concerts of classical music take place in the summer months in some of the historic interiors of Prague Castle. St. George's Basilica, the Ball-games Hall in the Royal Garden and the Spanish Hall and some of the rooms in Lobkowicz Palace serve as concert halls.

Short-term exhibitions are organized by the National Gallery in the Riding-school of Prague Castle and by Prague Castle intself in the so-called Imperial Stable, in the Theresian Wing, in the Royal Summer Palace and in other interiors. Signs and posters inform visitors to the Castle about exhibitions.

The reception rooms of Prague Castle are regularly accessible twice a year – in May and October. The precise date is published well in advance by the communication media.

PETR CHOTĚBOR
PRAGUE CASTLE
DETAILED GUIDE

Translation: Joy Turner-Kadečková
Photographs: Miroslav Hucek, Barbara Hucková
Drawings: Petr Chotěbor
Practical information: František Kadlec
Editing: Ljuba Horáková
Graphic design: František Obešlo
Publisher: The Prague Publishing House of Jiří Poláček
(Pražské nakladatelství Jiřího Poláčka)
in cooperation with BKT Alice Brindlerová
Printer: HELIOS, Exprint Červený Kostelec
Binding: Polygrafia Sadská
1994